THE UNNAMED KALIANA WAY

A MANUAL FOR THE INTERIOR LIFE

KEMPER KALIANA

outskirts
press

Outskirts Press, Inc.
http://www.outskirtspress.com

Paperback ISBN: 978-1-4787-7935-3
Hardback ISBN: 978-1-9772-0375-5

PRINTED IN THE UNITED STATES OF AMERICA

—————◆—————

To the growing community of students who are engaging this work with me, who encouraged me to write it all down so they could more easily remember, and who teach me as much if not more than I teach them: I learn more about myself from working with all of you than I ever could alone, and therefore, we are symbiotically entangled in a quantum classroom of cosmic proportion. The challenge of putting these concepts and pointers into words was not only a tremendous growing experience, but was also a great joy, knowing that the forever unfinished final product will enrich our local gatherings as well as benefit the collective in these dark and transformative times, now and into the future. Many, many graces.

Also a special thanks to Melissa Sachs: As though you weren't already, you can now be a part of something bigger than yourself. For your and Brian's financial contribution, I am forever grateful.

—————◆—————

Table of Contents

Advisory

---◆---

Self-publishing is a rewarding, "feel-good-about-yourself" accomplishment, with built-in benefits of freedom and independence, but an extremely challenging task. I learned a lot from my first publication process to implement this go-round, including the work it does on my OCD symptom of perfectionism. I proofread and edited it as thoroughly as possible without getting into a headspin, but there are sure to be things I overlooked. I would ask that you overlook those as well, and consider how the Five Basics presented here apply: for example, relative vs Ultimate (and how you interpret changeful words into Ultimate Truths, or grammar as having universal meaning for all time, especially if it seems "permanent" because of ink on a page or something you learned in school); also, if so-called imperfections "bother" you, it's an opportunity to ask why, and take back the projected conditioning of pointing out problems rather than appreciating the good. This has been my approach and my practice. I do take all of this very seriously; I just can't catch it all on my own. Don't worry, it's a damn good book, I'm damn proud of it, and this is not a cop-out or a defense. One day I may have an "editing team," but that will be far down the road, and they will need to deeply understand this information as well as my use of words and writing style. So no one jump the gun just yet. It will all unfold perfectly as always. I just wanted to "throw that out there" before you continue on.

The content of the "Unnamed Kaliana Way" is alive and evolving. While I am confident that its first official literary iteration, which you now hold in your hands, is complete unto itself, there is surely another volume to come. So hold it loosely (as with all things), looking as though through a multi-dimensinoal, ever-widening, upward-spiraling kaleidoscope. Receive and process the information, and practice the invitations, contextually, at the intersection of life circumstance, cultural climate, cognitive theory, and how far you want to take it. Supplement with the other books, videos, and guided meditations on my website, kgraykaliana.com (as well as the other authors and teachers that I recommend there), and be on the lookout for the 2nd edition of this one as it grows and matures and carves its own groove.

I am concerned with actual progress on the journey for those who are approaching my work for such purpose. In a watered-down world of too many gurus who do not equip their students to make traction, the Kaliana Container serves as a bona fide, tasted-and-tested, tried-and-true pot of ingredients that have worked for me, that I have seen work for others, that I therefore have assimilated into my being and do understand intimately, and that I can in good faith offer and suggest to you. The Container itself is always expanding as I continue to cut a path through the jungle of my own interior, safe enough for you to walk on. If it's outside of the Container, I simply can't make a sound judgement for its practical effects and results; because I don't know it myself. To be clear, the Kaliana Container includes all that was mentioned above: my books and videos, my guided audio meditation techniques, and the long list of other teachers, books, authors, videos, documentaries, etc. that I am continuously adding to (all of which can be found on my website).

Exploring the interior is what I do, at the edge of the uncharted. So this advisory is not intended to be exclusionary, dogmatic, or bigoted. It's for the students under my care who have been misguided for years with faux spirituality that not only produces no results, but often more suffering (this has, in fact, been reported to me directly). If you follow the living, kaleidoscopic mosaic in all of its utterances, you will not only glimpse inside my own mind, but you will join a rich and vibrant caravan, ancient in the making, wise in the working, and fresh in the Moment. I bid you welcome.

-Kemper

The way that can be walked is not the eternal Way
The word that can be spoken is not the eternal Word
The name that can be given is not the eternal Name
The Unnamed is the Only Real

All things begin and end
Clinging to what changes is suffering
This is only surface, form the outer shell
Not the way, not the Way
The Unknown is the Only Real

But not to walk is to be caught in quicksand
Not to speak is blasphemy
Not to name exalted ignorance
Naming and Unnaming are One
Knowing Unknowing the Same
Surface and deep, shell and inside
Begin and end in the common place

This place is no place
This Void full of form
Dark beyond dark
Night brighter than light
The path to all knowing
Undone and done again
The gate has been unhinged
Unattached and reimagined

Here at the end of the Age
Where warriors are called to grace
Heaven and earth crucified
In the alchemist's crucible fire
And what is born is Unbegotten

This is the Kaliana Way[1]

---

1   This poem is my own inspired rendition of *The Tao Te Ching* #1.

Preface

————◆————

Obviously "unnamed" is a name, and trying to *not* make a thing a thing makes a thing a thing. The Artist Formerly Known As... is what the artist was currently known as. So don't go there. I get questioned, "Well, why do you have to name it anything?," or, "They're just words anyway, right?" Puh-lease! There are a few reasons the name is un-named besides the nod to Lao tzu and the brilliant *Tao Te Ching*.[2] Let's get the "just words anyway" one out of the way first—I'm a writer. Words are my paint and brush, my raw material to shape a nothing into something; to give my innermost thoughts a form, an exterior expression and life. It need not be that way. I could still have the profound realizations and creative insights that I've had and not get it out there in this (or any, for that matter) medium. I like to tell my students that everyone who discovers the "True Self" (by whatever title) or has any unexpected experiences of the holy, of God, of the Ultimate Reality in all its formless forms, or whose paradigm shifts in such a radical way as to transcend cultural conditioning, preconceived biases, biological necessities, and psychological assumptions is compelled to *do something about it!*

For each it's different; for each it's unique. Some "sell their possessions," some leave the world for the monastic life, some start a non-profit, some serve in third-world countries, some donate money to the source that showed it to them, some (these days) start YouTube channels or vlogs, some do nothing...absolutely nothing... because all the somethings they'd been doing were perpetuating the problem and were the source of the suffering now ceased. Me? I write. I teach. I show what I've seen. I guide others to the same. And let's be clear: *Teacher* has come to mean so many things, especially in our

---

2   It is said that Lao Tzu did not write anything down, because he knew that as soon as he did, it would not only be meaningless, but already obsolete.

21st century kitschy, New Age, globalized, monetized, technologized spiritual culture. "This is my teacher" is a commonplace indication. It's even an accepted category of profession—"What do you do?" "I'm a spiritual teacher." These would be perfectly fine if we weren't so confused, and if we didn't have so many scandals of abuse at the hands of "spiritual teachers," and if we didn't give our power away to and worship on pedestals those we believe to have some special elite knowledge and symbolize a chasm of separation between the "common" person. It would also be acceptable if the majority of folks claiming to have multiple spiritual teachers and paths were actually making progress on the journey! There would be no problem either if the teachers themselves would not perpetuate the separateness and seek to boost their own image high in the sky of their "teaching."

I grew up in a religious milieu that laid out a story of an unbridgeable gap that humans, in their sinfulness, simply could not cross to get to Almighty Perfect God. The myth made Jesus the solution to the problem, because he was fully a man, but a sinless man, and he was fully divine, but a humble divine. Problem was, the formula goes that even so, Jesus is still unreachable, in a league of his own, better than everyone (despite his own words to the contrary, "Truly, truly, I say to you, he who believes in me will also do the works that I do; and greater works than these will he do..."[3]). And please don't get caught up on the word "believes"—this is precisely what I am referring to here as part of the problem. The Church wants "believes" to mean "buy into" the myth, the story, and the set of facts *about* Jesus. The original Greek Πιστεύω (pronounced pis-*stew*-o) meant something closer to "trust." Jesus was asking his people to *trust* him. Could you hear it differently, rather than the Magic/Mythic fairy tale version? "Guys, trust me! You'll be able to do all this and more if you do your practice. All I'm doing is showing you the way." I know all the objections. But save them until I'm finished. There was a Christian rock band back in the day that had a song: "Never gonna be as big as Jesus/Never gonna hold the

---

3   John 14:12, Revised Standard Version

world in my hands/Never gonna be as big as Jesus/Never gonna build a Promised Land/But that, that's alright, okay with me."[4] How much more obviously *contra* to what Jesus says in John 14:12 is that? And that's not even in any of the taboo texts, but right there in the good ol' fashioned Bible! Is anyone even listening?

Anyway. Back to our understanding and discussion of what a teacher is, and what I'm doing here. The word *teacher* has its origins in "to point out, present, or show." Unfortunately even the word guru—which has its Sanskrit roots in the same denotation, along with tones that mean "heavy," "weighty," "gravitas," pointing to someone who points out, presents, or shows things of significant concern or interest—has developed a connotation that implies separation, worship, and someone to whom you give your power away and must rely on for your awakening. When even St. Paul says, "May this mind be in you, which was in Christ Jesus, who, though he was in the form of God, did not count equality with God a thing to be grasped, but emptied himself, taking the form of a servant, being born in the likeness of men,"[5] what do you think he meant? If the *same mind* of one who was in the form of God *and* the form of humans is possible, then are we all not that?

Think about it. There is no sense of separation in this invitation from Paul. The separation came later in our dogmatic interpretation and fearful assumptions. Nicodemus comes to Jesus in the dark of night with a genuine desire and burning that he knew he must ask, seeing something in Jesus that he wanted to see for himself, whatever the

---

4   I hate to throw 'em under the bus, but I gotta give credit where credit's due and "cite my sources," yeah? That's Audio Adrenaline, and the song is called, you guessed it, "Never Gonna Be As Big As Jesus." Geez! Us!

5   Philippians 2:5-7. The Revised Standard Version, which I typically refer to, has "Have this mind among yourselves...," but the Greek is clearly more accurate to what's being said. The word ἐν is used, which clearly means "in," not merely "among." There is a major difference. The translators of the Revised Standard were probably scared to say what it really says because of the implications not only for the separative authoritarian Church, but also the responsibility that it would inevitably call all Christians to: namely, to be the same as Jesus.

risk, and Jesus tells him very practically how to (i.e., get rid of every identification with relative things, including your own personal, earthly life; never anything about worshipping him or believing a set of facts about him), but Nicodemus is too conditioned by his own thinking to get it.[6] So my role and goal as a teacher is simply this: to point out, for any who would genuinely want to see for themselves, what I have seen on the interior, spiritual journey; and to share what I have learned about God, liberation, healing, enlightenment, awakening, and what it means to be human.[7]

So that's what, if I'm *trying* to do or be anything, I'm trying to do and be. As for the premature quip that words have no meaning, and "Unnamed" doesn't mean anything anyway, and as soon as I write them they're outdated, that's a slap in the face of a writer whose primary purpose is to create meaning in order to transcend meaning. If you too quickly slip into meaninglessness from a nihilistic stance, you've lost the potential of meaning itself to be rocket fuel into something altogether *beyond* meaning (not *before* meaning).

It's *before—>become—>beyond.*[8] There is a time before you are a self; then you must become a self; then you must go beyond a self. There is a time before there is meaning; then you must find meaning; then you must go beyond meaning. There is a time before duality; then you must work with duality; then you must go beyond duality. Before. Become. Beyond.

When people started coming to me asking, like Nicodemus, what it is I see and know, and how they can see and know it too, naturally I needed to come up with some sort of system or formula (not as a rigid rule, but as a teaching tool) simply so that I could convey in a cohesive manner, and in a way that could be referred back to and

---

6   I have plans to write a book in which I provide new meaning and interpretation to some of the worn out Scriptures and theology we have been handed. So just stand by for that; don't get caught up so much on the details now, but hear what I'm saying, the point I'm making.

7   Et cetera et cetera yadda yadda ad infinitum. You know, all the typical words.

8   For Ken Wilber scholars, this is my own way of depicting what he calls the "pre/trans fallacy."

"memorized," my own practice, method, and realization. "Way" is obviously an intentional reference to Jesus, who, I believe, when he said, "I am the Way, the Truth, and the Life. No one gets to the Father except through me" was speaking *from* the transcendent, Ultimate Self, and not the personality Jesus self (or rather, by that time, the two had become One, and there was no difference), and was saying that everyone else *in that state* is the same thing, and that the Way to the Ultimate Reality, Heavenly Father Hologram as I call it, is *through that Me*. Or, could you hear it another way?: "What I'm teaching you is the way to truth and life, and how to realize Oneness with God."

The Unnamed Kaliana Way is a path that I have carved out by following the instructions, injunctions, and insights of many teachers before; and though I honor them always, I now have the machete in my hands and am hacking my own way through a wilderness, where they left off, making it clear for you to come along for as long as you like; as long as it's relevant and resonant for you, and then you're free to go off on your own when you're ready! Come—the Way is clear enough for you to walk! Use me as a reference like a field guide on a safari—I know where to take the group so that you can get the most out of your experience; I know where to point the binoculars; I know where the wild things hang out, the cute and cuddly things, the mysterious things, the strange things, and the hidden things. To say it another way: I see myself more like a classroom professor than a pedestaled master. I want to teach you "how" to do something I've learned to do, or teach you to see what I've come to see; teach you to understand what I know. Above all, I want to give you the tools to set yourself free, and to show you how to use them so that you don't have to rely on me beyond what you need. I want to eventually be your colleague, not your teacher. I want to share and compare notes with you as you do your own research. I want to see what you see! But first there may be some groundwork to do so that we're on the same page.

Some teachers have a need to not let their students "get it" so as to keep the authoritarian separation. There's a moment in the Stephen

Hawking movie, *The Theory of Everything*, in which his professor was now his proud peer, learning from him in his lecture hall. I want to deconstruct for you on the blackboard, so to speak, the finely working mechanism of the ego, to provide diagrams and models of "who you are," to dissect on the cutting board my own meditation practice and inner workings for you to see for yourself the constituent parts. That's what this book, and the work that I teach, is all about: priming the pump for actual discovery, and providing the most basic tools to get there and how to use them. In my own words, from my own perspective. My wife likes to say, tongue in cheek, that we didn't come here with a manual. She's right. But many have indeed provided what they feel are helpful instructions to at least survive, if not thrive, in whatever corner of the human experience they find most important. This is my valiant first attempt at such a tall, possibly impossible, order.

There are plenty of other teachers, field guides, and paths that work just fine; but just be weary of any who claim to always be ahead of the group with no chance of catching up. And be aware of mixing methods, simply because different teachers are not necessarily saying the same thing, but could be meaning wildly different things while using the same words. That's one reason I slow it down to define my terms, and also when appropriate make up my own, so that your mental conditioning doesn't quickly make a reference to a past (mis) understanding of a commonly used word like, say, false self or shadow or enlightenment. I want you to succeed in my course and go out into the world and teach your own in your own way, or implement what you learned unique to your vocation. I will also never stop my own work and exploration, so I'm happy for you to stay with me as long as you like and I will continue pointing and guiding. It's what I came here to do.

As for Kaliana. When Christy (my wife) and I got married, we both felt led to change our last name to something new altogether, for various reasons. Chief among them was that we have always known that we have come together in this life for a specific purpose and to create a new groove in the collective. Not only do we both understand ourselves to be "lineage healers," i.e., doing the transformative work for our respective ancestries that has not been done for many generations down the line, but moving forward, we are birthing a way of being that is unprecedented and rarely seen historically. Kaliana was a word we (thought we) made up, as a mash-up between *Kali* (the Hindu goddess originally known as the destroyer of evil) and *ana* (Greek for grace). We didn't realize the layers of meaning hidden for us, even further than what we intended (that I won't mention here) and just how perfectly it represented the vibration that we are seeking to emulate in our individual and together life. But the most significant surprise was the reminder that we are living in what the Vedas call the Kali Yuga, or Kalyuga, which is the densest, darkest, narrowest squeeze of a cycle after which another Golden Age is ushered in. There is much more to say about the Yugas, but there are also correlations in the book of Revelation, the Mayan calendar, and other ancient texts that imply we are living at the "end" of something significant before the birth of something even more significant. We did not have this in mind when we made our name Kaliana. But it's quite apropos to the work we do together, the work I'm presenting here, and the need (more than ever) for this work during such volatile, potent, and ripe-for-change times in our cosmic, global, political culture.

A Note As You're Reading

———— ◆ ————

This book was born from the request of one of my students who bravely asked during one of our in-person gatherings, when I must've been particularly rambling off the hook, "Are you going to write all of this down for us?" "Sure, I can do that," I said. I started the next day. The intention is that it be a comprehensive tour of my current understanding of what it takes to survive, and thrive, on the interior journey, as well as what I think the interior journey even is, because some have never even heard of such a thing! As such, my own thinking and teaching and practice of what is presented here is constantly evolving to meet the demands, questions, suggestions, and requests of my students and my own life. Therefore, maybe there is a 2.0 version up my sleeve down the road. But this is more than good for now.

I have chosen to write it in a more circular than linear fashion. By that I mean, the first time you read it, sure, read it straight through, start to finish; but thereafter, feel free to simply open it up and begin anywhere...like a magazine! (It's better than *People* I promise.) There may be concepts in the beginning chapter(s) that are new when you first come upon them that are then answered later on. So it's set up so that even if you don't understand something right off, by the end of the book you will, and in subsequent reads (if you dare!) it will only go deeper.

One of my primary concerns as a teacher in this field in our 21st century spiritual milieu is to parse out commonly used (and oft-cliche but actually appropriate) terms so as to be as clear as possible what I mean by them. Therefore, I have broken the chapters down into sub-subjects that can be easily flipped to by glancing at the table of contents. The style of writing is notably different from the more poetic or artistic renderings in, for example, *From Nowhere to Now-Here* (at the time of this writing, the first volume of that series has been published, with plans that the second will be out by the end of the current year, 2019 or beginning of next). So don't expect this to be same as that. While meant to be a textbook of sorts, it's still Kemper, and I have chosen a casual, though that doesn't mean shallow, conversational style and tone that I hope keeps it interesting and engaging. (I gots lotsa genres up my sleeve.)

I have also included quite a few "chapter notes" at the end of the book indicated by the superscript number (above the text). I chose these to be notes rather than included in the main text because they are, though not more advanced, more technical in nature, and a deeper cut. So, the following is a suggestion for how to engage the notes, that Ken Wilber makes in his books, for the reader, that I've always thought is a great idea: If you so choose, you can omit the notes and not miss any of the meaty content; or, you may read it through without the notes the first go-round, and then read it again with the notes the next go-round. Or just suck it up and read the notes from the get-go. The notes are not merely whimsical "options," but indeed are a bit more dense. So I would encourage you to give it a try at some point. I just know folks get overwhelmed, particularly with a more academic kind of text like this, so I'd rather you be more comfortable than brain-fried, while at the same time challenging your cognitive, and reading, capacity.

Here's how I do it with 700-page Ken Wilber books with hundreds of additional pages of chapter notes at the end (you might try it this way): Have two bookmarks—one to hold your place in the main text, and one to hold your place in the notes. When you come upon a note in the main text, simply stop, turn to the back bookmark, and read the note. If the note is square in the middle of a sentence, finish the sentence, and then read the note (for the note could be specifically referring to a particular word within the sentence, and not the whole sentence itself). This is really good training for those of you who claim to be slow readers or slow cognitive processors. The discipline of reading, as I've said, is a dying one, and is as important as ever, with our attention span dropping by the collective second. Reading is different from listening to an audiobook or watching a YouTube video, and reading a physical book is different from reading an ebook. Try it out. It matters to me that you do, and I promise it will also enhance your interior muscles for meditation (which, if you don't already know, is one of our Five Basics covered here!). It also requires that you slow down and take the time to read, another important aspect of the interior journey—slowing down to take time for practice. So, stretch your mind to hold the train of thought from the main text as you go to the note in the back, and then return, completing the thought, and registering the reason why I made a note to begin with.

Also, if there is a word you've never heard before, or are not sure what it means, and it's not a word that I'm in the process of defining for you, don't gloss over it! Pause your reading and look it up! Google is wonderful for being a dictionary. But don't get lost down the wormhole of the web simply because you did one search. Come back to the book. This may seem menial, but I know how the mind works these days—how easily distracted—and this book is entering precisely in that context.

If it's helpful, imagine me reading it to you. Hear my voice. Connect with my consciousness *as though* you're listening to me speak; for it is coming *from* me, and I am in fact delivering it *to* you. This is a way we can commune and converse. No need to worry about your pace, either. I remember when I was first devouring and digesting Ken's work, I would read maybe two pages over thirty minutes, and read and re-read whole paragraphs over again. Or I would stop at the end of a sentence and let it sink in before going on to the next. What if your gauge for how fast to read was your digesting, assimilating, and integrating (at least cognitively) of the material rather than simply how fast you can scan over words of the English language and get nothing from them; actual digestion, like eating. One bite at a time, and as long as it takes for it to really sink in. Again, it doesn't have to make total sense all at once, because this is a process of growth; but the true reception of the words and concepts into the soil of your self is of utmost importance.

The practice of reading itself is a kind of meditation, and requires a similarly relaxed, attentive, not distracted, focused-but-not-strained mental muscle engagement. A final exercise that I do when I'm reading, and that you might find helpful, is to not only underline key words and sentences, but to write in the margins your thoughts *about* the text, as though having a dialogue with the words, or with *me!* For this is a conversation between us through the medium of words on a page. Pretty cool. I never actually go back and read what I wrote in the margins, though you might, but I imagine as though the author of the book I'm reading were sitting in front of me, and I write elaborate questions, critiques, and my own thoughts alongside theirs in the sidebar, and continue back and forth until the ingestion is complete enough to move on to the next sentence. That's why Ken's 700-pagers take me something like nine months to a year to read. But I'm a different person when I'm finished, that's for sure. Talk about a relationship, talk about discipline! But it's incredibly rewarding, and I can actually *feel* my interior consciousness *growing, expanding,* real-time, as I do. These are just suggestions to try out, if they feel resonant, from my own experience. Let's give a warm welcome back to reading y'all!

Introduction

Me & Meditation

Me and meditation go way back. But it hasn't always been what it is today. In fact, I think my first introduction was when I was eight, on my psychologist's couch as he guided me through awareness of different parts of my body in an effort to relax each one. No doubt he also was responsible for turning my attention "inward" and making me a career introspector and writer.

For one of the primary compulsions that drove my mom crazy was that my obsessive thoughts would drive me out of bed ten times or more every night before I could fall asleep to tell her, to confess to her, to check with her, to remind her various and sundry objects of my mental rumination—to please not forget to pack two napkins, folded this certain way, in my lunchbox tomorrow; that I'm sorry I didn't brush my teeth the right way before bed; that I may have had the thought, "Mom's stupid"; that I just dreamed something that I forgot now; that thank you for being the best mom in the world; that I may have said my prayers out of order; that I was afraid of going to hell... For a fuller, more complete list (cuz that ain't the half of it), I plan to write another book in the future about my experience, specifically, with OCD.

In any case, I can only imagine her talking to the good doctor behind closed doors: "Can you *please* help him with this insane bedtime ritual so that we both can get some sleep!" So, one of his suggestions—which I later learned came from what's called "behavioral therapy," and which I can only imagine has one of the lowest success rates for anyone suffering from obsessive-compulsive disorder[1]—was that I resist the urge to get out of bed two minutes, then five minutes, then ten minutes, then twenty minutes, and so on until the onslaught of intrusive thoughts went away and I could drift quietly into dreamland. *Resist? Really doc? Yeah right! Have you ever had the OCDemon in your head telling you what to do? Try it and tell me how resisting works for you!* Instead of getting out of bed, the exercise was to write down everything I wanted to tell Mommy on a scrap piece of paper on my nightstand and I could show them all to her in the morning. Didn't help anything except her get more sleep, and me become an obsessively introspective writer. And now you get to see inside the brain born as a result in these books!

So I kept a notepad and/or torn up squares of paper by my bed with a pen and a flashlight and wrote *all* that I mentioned above *and more* (basically *everything* that swarmed into my mind, wanted or unwanted). Sometimes I wouldn't even bother turning the flashlight on because I had to get the thought out quickly to stop the torture and didn't have time to fight with the light which left a mess of scribbles that only I could decipher when my mom and I had our morning meetings. A common repetition (and I still have some of the papers to prove it) was that I would write the reminder, the obsession, the confession, the scruple, whatever, and then draw an arrow from it over to a secondary note that said either, "See me in the morning," or just, "See me." See me. See me. See me was everywhere. Nobody understood, nobody knew how to help.

Nobody could see me. It was my encoded SOS signal that was simply not meant to be heard until years and years and years later by a deeper Intelligence, an ancient Wisdom, a primordial practice buried in the sands of my own subconscious. Bless their hearts, my family, my doctors, my spiritual mentors did the best they could; but in the early 90s, the conservative South knew nothing about meditation, proper diet, yoga, ego, shadow, subpersonalities, trauma, energy work, mystical experience leading to psychotic breaks, neuroplasticity, herbal supplements, and everything I would later discover on my own to not only kick the habit of the pharma, but literally transform and heal the "mental disability" altogether.

Many of you have already heard that what I believe[2] caused (or, perhaps *triggered* a predisposition in my family's DNA) the onset of OCD was a profoundly mystical experience that happened when I was seven years old. The reason I don't share the full story very often is a few reasons. One, I am still unpacking, to this day, both cognitively (i.e., gaining more understanding and perspective "from where I now am" and from what I've studied) as well as physical-energetical-emotional-mental-spiritually, what happened. And two, I risk on the one hand saying too much, and on the other, not saying enough. Because, on the surface, when I tell the story of what happened exteriorly, it sounds both otherworldly as well as uneventful; skeptics could and would try to explain it away, and New Age romantics could and would give it too much weight. On the one hand, there are characteristics that point to an extra-terrestrial visitation, and on the other, the straight-up, good-ole Holy Spirit. I do have my mother as a witness, however. And for that I'm grateful.

What I do know is that the day after, when I returned to my 2nd grade classroom, the fluorescent lights in the hallway were noticeably brighter (the janitors had not been up all night changing the bulbs), and I was noticeably sensitive to their vibration; I felt "different" for the first time, and ostracized from my classmates (whereas the day before I was kind of a normal, albeit well-behaved and "sweet," sensitive kid); I suddenly had developed an unusual-for-my-age interest in God, reading my Bible, and going to church; and finally, the shadow...my very first real OCD symptom began only a few weeks thereafter. I won't fill in all the gaps of the story here (each of my books provide pertinent pieces of the mosaic, so if you read them all you'll get it all, or close to it).

Point is, these two serpents—the light of God Consciousness and the shadow of mental disorder—intertwined and determined my path for the next fifteen years.[3] What ensued was an all-out "war inside" with pharmaceuticals, psychiatrists, addiction, and anxiety in the mouth of one serpent, and bright-eyed curiosity, questions about spiritual matters that no parent or mentor could answer, a beyond-the-box gifted mind, and an unusually authentic "personal" relationship with Jesus Christ in the mouth of the other.

One of the countless other shades and varieties of OCD that manifested over the years was scrupulosity (an actual clinically recognized "type" of OCD), which interestingly enough I learned was first noticed and documented in the 1600s among certain monks whose conscientious zeal tipped overboard into obsessive, intrusive thoughts of guilt and wrongdoing that would only be alleviated by a compulsion to confess, repent, and practice severe penitential punishments.[4] More on my monk story in other books, but there is certainly a connection, most likely to a past life, and to the correlation between the "religious" experience and the onset of the "disorder." My mind was filled with uncontrollable checks and balances to be sure that I did not offend anyone, make God angry, or commit even the slightest accidental "sin"; and if I did find something that I *may* have done (even if I was not sure, even if inadvertent), then a whole litany of compulsive prayers of confession and repentance would occupy my mind for the next few minutes, or even hours, and I would not feel clear until I also confessed to the person directly whom I may have wronged (it was usually met with a raised brow that I would even admit to having done such a miniscule thing, or the person would not have even given whatever-it-was a second thought; "Yeah, sure, I forgive you. Anything else?" was usually the typical response).

Included with this was a terrifying fear of hell and incessant, racing thoughts taking the form of mental prayers to God about everything under, and beyond, the sun. Even as I started making progress on other symptoms, there was a time I wondered if this one in particular would ever go away—it was almost *pre*-autonomous, meaning rooted more deeply than any other autonomous function of the body, i.e., breath, heartbeat, thought itself. Sub-subconscious. But, with time, with patience, with practice...well, let's just say I wouldn't be writing this book if it were not completely gone. I remember the moment that it left. It was kind of one of those "woke up one day and everything was different" experiences: yesterday my mind was racing, today it's clear, and it's never started up again. Simple as that.

I also had what I call "Tourette's face." One of my many psychologists once gave me a valuable piece of information (it wasn't *all* for nothing after all): that studies have shown Tourette syndrome to be a "cousin" of obsessive-compulsive disorder. This made, and makes, a lot of sense. Most of my childhood, I had a plethora of facial tics that caused not an insignificant amount of discomfort and even pain.

There was this eyeball muscle tensing thing that I did that made my vision go blurry and caused others to ask if I was okay. And you know that little connective tissue that holds your tongue to the bottom of your mouth? Mine is a little more prominent than average, and I would slip that baby between my middle two teeth until it was swollen and raw. Opening my mouth as wide as it would go until I felt a certain "stretch" in the corners, or until the corners split open—that's another. Furrowing or raising (or both at the same time) my brow, scrunching my nose, and making my ears move back and forth, grinding my teeth and clenching my jaw—all with a particular (though involuntary) rhythm and pattern, until it felt complete, until it happened again. On and on and on. And I remember the day, the moment, when all of these just didn't happen anymore. There are still sometimes very slight and subtle movements of facial muscle that could be categorized as tics (and you can even catch me blinking with a hard squeeze every now and then), but again, nowhere close to what it was, and nothing that I would now call "Tourette's face." And I give all the credit to the work put forth in this book.

Last thing for now. Having been "downloaded" with a lightning bolt of high vibration as a seven-year-old, I believe it went straight to my root chakra as a ball of unrealized, molten, hot potential, and when the serpent decided to start growing up (this is my Eastern influence speaking now), it got to 2nd chakra genital-sexual-umbilical development, and became twisted and distorted due to lack of understanding, training, and teaching from my "mentors," mixed with the taboo, sin, and guilt associated with sex in general. That energy had to go *somewhere*, and because the intensity in my mentally disabled mind was so loud, I needed not only physical and energetic release, but I also needed a projector screen to reflect back that I was indeed as bad and sinful as the Church said I was. I remember thinking, as a child soaking up this stuff like a sponge, "I don't feel like a sinner," "I don't think I'm a bad person, but they say I am, so I guess I have to be that before Jesus will forgive me." Deeply psychologically twisted.

So from about age 15 to 25, I became a full-blown addict of...thanks to our millennial milieu providing ease of access to such things...pornography, websites for one-night hookups, and other fixes too dark to mention here. I even went to 12-Step Sex Addicts Anonymous meetings as a 20-something-year-old—with all the old guys who had ruined their marriages. Anyway. Nothing helped except, you guessed it, meditation, yoga, spiritual practice, all of the above, mentioned above. I was delivered (thanks be to God) finally and fully at age 25 from all of it, kind of all at once—addiction, OCD, medication, etc. And the serpent of light was allowed to grow up through more highly evolved chakras and not bound up and suppressed and distorted at 2nd.

When I would stay up until five a.m. frying my retinas with the blue light of pornographic images in my college dorm, or across the hall from my parents' bedroom, I would fall asleep to the sunrise with my favorite worship music from my laptop by my pillow sweetly singeing EMFs into my brain to soothe the guilt. Then I would wake up a few hours later with an abysmal pit in my stomach and a panicked pang: "Oh my God what did I do last night? How much money did I spend? Did I call someone? Did I go somewhere?" And shuffle over to the coffee pot, pour a cup, sit at my desk, journal about God's love, grace, and forgiveness, and my sinfulness and brokenness, read the Bible or other devotional book, pray[5] and ask the Lord to please deliver me from this hell. Then go to class and nod off from lack of sleep and the little pink pill now swimming in my bloodstream. It was hell indeed.

But I never once (and have never once) turned my back on "my first love," that Golden Serpent of Light that kissed me in my bedroom when I was but a baby, now winding its way, kundalini-like, with greater intensity and a mind of its own, an agenda of its own, that I had no choice but to hang onto for dear life, dear death, 'til we came to our next destination. Every one of my prayers that I have ever prayed has been answered. But God's timing is not always what we'd like it to be—at first at least, for when we learn the work, and learn how to work with God, and let God work on us, everything comes to pass as it should, and all darkness is perfectly part of the entire unfolding; all sins forgiven, all wounds healed, all littleness transcended, all separateness sealed, all fragments wholled. Truly.

One of the profoundly unexpected graces along the way was the discovery of yoga and meditation, in the South, where such things in an authentic, quality environment are hard to come by (at least they were in 2008). I landed right in the lap of the perfect studio where a brother and sister duo, Lynn and Jacob Felder (she taught the yoga, he the meditation) were just what I needed to get going. Jacob's "Awareness Approach," as he calls it, was the first to provide the basic nuts and bolts of how to engage and focus and strengthen interior muscles.[6] What I soon found, and felt, and experienced directly, especially surprising because I didn't necessarily know what I was getting myself into (Lynn simply told me once, "I think you'd like Jacob's meditation class," so I tried it out), and because I didn't have any experience with meditation before, which is sad having been raised with such religious zeal (shouldn't my religious teachers have taught me, a bright-eyed eager spiritual infant, how to meditate? But alas, that's a lament for another time...), and because his Awareness Approach had zero spiritual decorations or fluff (he just wanted to teach us how to consciously relax our body while keeping the mind awake, and to maintain awareness in between waking and sleeping) that this would be the beginning of the "return" path to Union with the God who "began a great work in me"[7] at age seven (or lifetimes ago).

As yoga was blowing my mind through the sacred connection with my physical body, meditation was blowing my mind by the new worlds of exploration, the new domain of experience, and the new silence and stillness immenanting and rippling through every cell of my being. I would soon "graduate" from Jacob's method (he didn't have any such distinction; I'm merely using that word myself) and discovered Centering Prayer, a contemporized version (made so by Father Thomas Keating and others) of a medieval monastic method put forth in the classic book *The Cloud of Unknowing*. Though I never "turned my back" on Jesus when I discovered the world of yoga, I didn't realize at the time that there was in fact an entire contemplative, meditative, ascetic, transformative, practice-based tradition right in the Christian storehouse; it's tucked away, covered in dust and rust in the attic somewhere, but it's there nonetheless. It felt like returning to the Home I'd never been to after being raised in a halfway house. But again, having found such depth in the East, neither did I turn my back on what I learned there, either. I couldn't. I had to now incorporate both. Jacob's pragmatic approach helped train my mind for meditation and prep me for the dive I was about to take into the esoteric and multi-perspectival waters of many true authentic traditions. I was "transcending and including," becoming Integral before I even knew what such things were. My sphere was becoming wider, my God becoming greater, my Self becoming richer, my path becoming clearer by the ever-unfolding Present Moment.

The Basics

I'll suspend the "story" here, the gestalt to be continued in other books. Concluding for now, the pieces were starting to come together, not only for my own personal healing, transformation, and liberation, but also in preparation for the day that I would be teaching and assisting others on the journey. I have known from a very young age that this is what I came here to do, and had already gotten my feet wet with various leadership roles in the Church, but I had no idea the breadth and depth of information I would stumble upon "outside the box," subsequently assimilate into my system, and be inspired and readied to transmit.

So, fast-forward through about ten years of what I call "false starts" or "trial runs" (i.e., platforms and venues and weekly classes and a failed blog and yoga studios and workshops) in which my inherent question was always, "Is this it?" "Is now the time?" "Is it happening?" The answer was always, well yes and no—for there's never a "time" when it "starts," you also don't ever actually "retire" from this field if it's genuine, and in this work there's no such thing as dress rehearsal or practice (especially if it's to the public, because if people are listening, it's for real; you're either teaching the material or not).[8] Of course, if it's not always evolving and being refined, then it's a dead, out-of-context, rigid system or set of rules to follow; but from the jump I never wanted to be "kind of" teaching. I wanted to make sure I got the full okay from the Universe, God, Higher Wisdom, Intuition, what-have-you before I jumped the gun and said a bunch of things I wasn't stable enough to support.

I have also always been aware of the pitfalls of teaching this material from an egoic place, so my early years were spent making sure I wasn't doing anything for fame or recognition or money. I'm glad I did, so that now there is no chance of a shadow rearing its head in that regard. My early journals are full of, you might say, self-micro-managing thoughts to not let any pride or arrogance or false humility or ego take the reins. If someone praised me for an inspirational sermon, I would not say thank you but would give the praise back to God and be on close lookout that their comment did not get lodged in my psyche as a narcissistic "look at me" loop. Now that I have deconditioned myself from the need on the one hand to deflect admiration and gratitude and on the other hand the need to need it (both of which lots of teachers struggle with), I just say thank you and move on.[9]

Finally, over the past year-and-a-half-ish as of the time of this publication, a ripening has occurred, in which the momentum of my own journey, a firm rooting of the realizations that I teach, and an autonomous voice rather than one that merely parrots others has produced a seedbed of students who are listening and learning, a cultural context ready for the work, and a lovely location to gather in. We are a rapidly growing and maturing community, and true transformation is already taking place.

It didn't take long to realize, however, that not only was it important that I make clear the specific vibration and approach that I am coming from (because, especially in our town, every teacher of spiritual work has their own unique perspective, and just because we all use the word "ego" or "shadow" or "awakening" or "transformation" or "enlightenment" or "true self" or "awareness" does not mean we mean the same thing). I am not saying my way is *better*, but I am saying it's *specific*, and the container I'm holding is at least Integral, which is vastly different from anything less, so I would call all "spiritual teachers" to clarify for their students just what it is they're saying, and not take for granted or assume that everyone is on the same page or "just saying the same thing in a different way." Trust me, I'm learning this from experience.

So, as we started gathering, it seemed important that I condense my teaching down to what I call the Five Basics, and that's precisely what this book is about. Each Basic has its own chapter, and each chapter has sub-subjects that break it down even further. The Basics, as you'll see, are the bare minimum of what's required to survive, and thrive, on the human interior journey. Speaking of which, there is an entire chapter dedicated to what "interior" means to begin with. In the same way as there are basic skills learned as children to be human on the exterior (such as cooking, brushing your teeth, going to the bathroom, taking care of yourself when you're sick or injured), why are we not taught the same for being human on the interior (such as how to handle the ego, understanding projection, navigating emotions, and eliminating psycho-spiritual suffering)? Once you've grown up exteriorly, then you can go exploring—you can become a concert pianist, learn to climb mountains, compete as an athlete, or build houses. Same on the interior. There are limitless worlds and uncharted territories to be discovered and enjoyed. But there is a pre-requisite training period and an entire vocabulary to become proficient in before you go off on your own. Unfortunately, we are all born into a culture (at least for now) that overemphasizes the exterior to the detriment of the interior; and though we look like adults on the outside, we are infants inside until and unless we do the work in that terrain too.

With that said, and to reiterate, these are the Basics of the interior human life, as I see them, from where I now sit, arising "smack-dab" in the middle of the world we live in. And I've learned over the past year-plus that, though I can go off on tangential vines and branches for days and not run out of stuff to talk about, these Five can never be exhausted or returned to often enough. The roots must be established, and established again. I've also learned that though I say the words with my mouth, it doesn't mean they land and register in the minds and hearts of my listeners the way that I want them to or think they do. This is another reason that I was glad to comply with the request of writing it all down. Take this book as saying "what it is I'm trying to say" in the form of a few basic principles for your knapsack along the way. Which means, the Five Basics is simply a pedagogical tool, and not an unbending, universal system for all time, nor a "lifestyle" that you have to follow (but in its very Integral malleability, I do think it's pretty good). What's more, I will never ask anyone to practice anything I have not already tested on (and approved of) myself; while again, always updating, upgrading, and expanding as I blaze the trail of my own path. This points to the value of the website, my videos, and regular in-person meetings with the group (if you're local). So once you're in, stay tuned and grow *with* me!

Before we go further, here are The Basics (in the order they appear in the book, but I put them in no particular order, of importance or any other):

- Meditation Practice

- The Ultimates

- Taking Responsibility

- Who Am I? (& who am I not?)

- Interior Domain

The Work

I feel it is important to mention that when I say "the work," as I often do, I am not referring to the trademarked term coined by Byron Katie. While not altogether different from her "Work" in the sense of a deeply honest and transformational interior inquiry (which she would agree with), it's just not the same system. And since I've brought her up, I should say that I've only been lightly introduced to her work with "The Work," and don't have much of an opinion either way about it. Therefore she's not on my list of influences. But I wanted to bring this to your attention for the sake of, again, keeping the container clear and delineating the difference (because though we are in the same ballpark, the ballpark is big, and are most certainly not sitting in the same seat). When I say "the work," I mean something less technical and something more like the committed implementation and consideration of the Five Basics and their constituent parts on a moment-to-moment as well as structured, regimented basis.

Since we're on the subject, work is not a nice word these days, of course. It reminds us of corporate offices and taxes and money and that thing we have to do that we'd usually rather not do. I hope none of those associations are made when we talk about the world of the work in this book. Eventually, there is a transition point into enjoyability when work of any kind is approached like cultivating a skill, a craft, or an art. The finished product you not only love, but the process of the creation, as well as fine-tuning to a level of mastery, if you are motivated enough.

I like using the analogy of a garden; but not everyone loves gardening (in fact, I don't even love gardening, but it's a great metaphor), so think of your favorite pastime or hobby or sport (on the exterior) that requires patience, effort, attention, and practice to get really good at it. Remember when the effort finally paid off? Remember when it became effortless? Remember when one day you were able to put your own spin on it and not just copy your teacher? Remember when maybe you started teaching others too? Remember when practicing became fun and not a chore? That's what I mean. On the one hand, this is just like that because it requires repetition and a whole new set of muscles, so to speak, to "get it," and it is something you can become proficient at, with checkpoints of progress along the way. On the other hand, it's nothing like that, because the very desire to accomplish something or get a prize or achieve a goal, while a good motivator at first is usually the very thing, in this arena, that prevents the eager beaver ego from giving up control and allowing the ardent traveler to complete the journey.

In any case, let's pretend you love to garden. A garden is a great analogy, and, I have found, is a very archetypal image that is used in other traditions as well for various illustrations. Consider the steps required: First you have a hard, dry, cracked piece of earth with weeds and bramble bushes and overgrowth that you must spend dedicated time clearing out and tilling. This in and of itself is grunt-work, and a novice gardener might easily give up if they don't keep the reward of the final product in mind. Even along the way, once the garden is in full glory, it is necessary to continue pulling weeds and keeping it nicely cultivated—this can be akin to returning to your practice regularly, putting in the work, as sort of maintenance like other exterior hygiene (you just do it). Pulling weeds can itself become enjoyable if it's in the warm sunshine alongside a partner with birds singing and a gentle breeze. Tilling the soil is correlated with, at the beginning, a constant and steady re-training of the mind and the interior sensitivities to a new way of seeing and being. With our current conditioned impatience and need for instant gratification, when the results are not yet paying off, it's easy for us to get discouraged quickly. So at the beginning, even more trust and perseverance and looking to others whose gardens are thriving as a reminder of where you want to be and can be and will be one day is crucial.

The seeds can represent the particular *kind* of garden you want to have. What do you want to grow? St. Paul says the *fruit of the spirit* is love, joy, peace, patience, kindness, goodness, gentleness, faithfulness, and self-control.[10] These are not "commandments" or rules or things to try and do—why else would he call them *fruit*? Fruit is the *natural* result of hard work (and a cooperative effort between the gardener and Mother Earth). These, he's saying, are by-products of the spiritual journey. They can be gauges for progress as well, i.e., along the way, are you becoming more loving? more peaceful? more joyful? more patient? more kind (to yourself and others)? is goodness shining from your being? more gentle? more faithful to your practice? and more aware of your self, thoughts, words, and actions? Then you are bearing good fruit. In the Yogic and Hindu traditions, there is a concept called *Satcidananda* which is three Ultimates strung together into one word—Being *(Sat)*, Consciousness *(Cid)*, and Bliss *(Ananda)*—and is said to be what is attained when one realizes "Brahman" or the Ultimate Reality. In the *Tao Te Ching,* chapter 16, it says, "[As a result of the work], you naturally become tolerant, disinterested, amused, kindhearted as a grandmother, dignified as a king...you can deal with whatever life brings you, and when death comes, you are ready."[11] You will come to see that all the traditions, in their esoteric, experiential, trans-formational versions have a kind of three step path—(1) Recognize and be honest about suffering, (2) Implement a specific practical method as a means to eliminate it, and (3) Live in the liberated expansion that comes when suffering is gone.

The seeds that you plant in your now fertile and receptive soil, therefore, if we take the analogy further, come from fruit that has already gone through the process (or, from teachers, fellow travel-ers, other sources, of whose fruit you have tasted and can confirm that theirs is something you'd like to grow in your garden). So you ask them to plant seeds or give you seeds from their yield. Heirlooms they're called. Or purebreds in the animal world.

Jesus tells a parable popularly called "The Parable of the Sower" that coalesces nicely with the analogy of planting seeds for the interior life. It's found in three of the four canonical gospels, so it seems very likely that it was authentically attributed to him. It speaks of a sower planting seeds that land in different kinds of soil, each with different outcomes. I'll paraphrase. You imagine someone grabbing big hand-fuls from their bag and throwing seeds randomly across the ground, spreading them all around. Some, Jesus says, land on the road where they get trampled by foot traffic and where the terrain is too hard to take the next step of sprouting. Some, Jesus says, land on the side of the road, where there's a little more cushion and potential, but the crows come and snatch up the seeds before they even have a chance. Some, Jesus says, land in receptive soil, even start to sprout and take root, but they are surrounded by too many vines and weeds that have already taken up residence there, so they soon get choked out when they've just gotten started. Some, finally, Jesus says, land in the perfect plot of fertile soil that has been cultivated and is ready. So the seeds sprout, take root, grow, bloom, and blossom into full fruition, which then of course (as we said above, and now I'm taking the parable further) produce more seeds which are pollinated and carried by the wind to other lands and the process begins again. Some never have a chance, some get started and don't finish, and some make it to their full potential as beautiful vegetation.

You can draw the parallels from here yourself. Point is, it requires the right environment, cultivation, dedication, patience, time, more time, more time, "sun," "water," "earth," "wind" (and what these represent in the parable), intelligence, wisdom, trust, prayer, and a little luck.[12] Eventually the garden comes to full bloom and the reward is far worth the work. The work continues, but as I already said, it's more like routine, rhythmic maintenance, which itself is enjoyable and a reward for its own sake. Now the gardener and the garden (i.e., you and God) are both in accordance with "nature" and can work together— or, my will and the Father's are one (again, paraphrasing Jesus). Stick with it. It will come. I promise. And follow my guidance for as long as it's relevant.

The Traditions

One of my greatest drives in this life is to return the cliche, run-of-the-mill, popularized, shallow, watered-down interpretation and expression of the authentic, ancient, esoteric, contemplative paths to their originally-intended depth so that they make sense in the context and consideration of our current experience of being human (and with an eye to the evolution of consciousness), while at the same time being mindful that such an upgrade does not lose their profound quality and truly transformational potential, as many such "contemporizations" do. In many ways, I'm "old fashioned"—I do not have social media, I still handwrite my journals in cursive with pen and ink, I do not use electronic assistance in my meditation—no bells and whistles—and I prefer an organic approach to the now popularized, and often distracting, supplementation of so-called plant medicine. At the same time, I am of the millennial generation (slightly proud, slightly ashamed to say), which makes such a trajectory that much more challenging when surrounded by others of my age that seek the spiritual fireworks and quick-fixes (that in fact do not work). So, as an old-fashioned, millennial teacher (a contradiction in terms in and of itself), I do my best to consider, integrate, and marry the best of all paths, while keeping clear and carving my own.

What do I mean by *authentic, ancient, esoteric, contemplative paths?* All the religions have an inner and an outer version; an institutionalized exterior and an initiatory interior; a dogmatic and a pragmatic expression. In a way, it's the *religious vs. spiritual* question (which has only gained a place in conversation recently, when some of the collective has grown beyond the confines of its Mythic adolescence yet still wants to partake in the essence of the traditions), but unfortunately, even these words have lost their meaning and value. After all, *religion* comes from the Latin *religare* which means something like "to connect" or "to bind together" or "to unite" (not much different from the meaning of the word *Yoga* in Sanskrit believe it or not, which is close to our English word *yoke* (no, not eggs)). So, even the outward-facing religions with their rules and rigidity and control have their roots in the soil of genuine spirituality. In my opinion, the founders, or first seers, of each religion were simply so ahead of their time (and therefore very misunderstood) that when they died, their followers had every best intention to carry on the torch, but simply ran into more division than unity, and rather than continuing the liberating practices that changed their life forever in the first place fell victim to fear and competition and ended up crystalizing the living path into a dead and boring (and even quite damaging) road.

Nonetheless, the fire does not die so easily. Hidden somewhere in the attic of each of the religions, buried beneath all the rulebooks, lies a still-beating heart that has silently and steadily made its way through thousands of years of conflict and turmoil. These are the paths of true experiential transformation, of practices and pointers so that anyone who aptly applies them can see first-hand what the first seers saw, can know directly what the masters knew. Buddhism has Zen; Judaism has Kabbalah; Christianity has Contemplative; Hinduism has Yoga; Islam has Sufism. This is a basic list, and there are more (the family tree has many branches), but you get the idea.

For the sake of having a fresh set of phrases, and not sticking with the same ole "spiritual vs. religious" distinction (or what some call esoteric vs. exoteric), from here on I will call the outward-facing institutional version of the religions the *exterior traditions*, and the in-ward-looking initiatory version the *interior traditions*. In general (and I really do mean broadly general), the exterior traditions are saying wildly different things, which is one reason (and only one reason) why they are always at odds and causing wars and killing members of the "others" (I could say more, but that's another side trail altogether), and the interior traditions are saying basically the same thing, which is: *There is a way to heal all wounds and find liberation, peace, and joy. Here's how...* The "here's how" is what's different for each of the interior traditions, but those differences are not nearly as detrimental as the differences on the exterior; in fact, not detrimental at all. They are merely different textures and ways of using the given imagery of the culture, era, and world in which the tradition was born (as I'm doing now). I do not mean "merely different" to indicate an "it-doesn't-matter" sameness. They each are saying the same thing in their own beautiful language.[13] For example, the Contemplative Christian tradition has an entirely different perspective on and practical approach to suffering, karma, and the Ultimate Reality (or God) than the Zen Buddhist (for Jesus and Siddhartha themselves both had different experiences of these). Which is why, as I am honing in on what it is I am trying to say, what it is I teach, what it is I see, what it is I believe (and acknowledging the occasions when what I see and what I believe may themselves be different—seeing is direct, believing is conjecture. Everyone has a belief system, even if not stuck in the swamp of the exterior tradition; and at the same time, seeing and believing play on each other), I utilize and draw from the many influences and flavors and teachers and traditions and mentors that have shaped who I am as a learner and practitioner, and therefore as a teacher.

Healing & Liberation

I cannot overemphasize that, from my perspective and in my experience, each of the Five Basics is okay on its own but incomplete without all of the others for the full process of healing and liberation. For example, a meditation practice requires an understanding of the Ultimates; shadow work on the finite self requires the Who Am I? inquiry; the interior domain is accessed by meditation but is not the same kind of "mental preparation" a triathlete practices before a race; boundless I Am-ness requires healthy boundaries to express itself through; liberating Oneness needs deep healing of the ego or else the transcendent realization becomes a contracted narcissistic trip; taking back projection requires the knowledge that there is ultimately no exterior world or objective "other" onto which to project in the first place, and the discovery that there is no objective "other" onto which to project in the first place requires the responsibility not to carelessly hurt those in your field of Alone Awareness.

For me (and there are many ways to say it), healing is clearing out the debris from who you were, and liberation is expanding into who you are. Both must be included, as goals to aim for as well as gifts to receive, but they are neither linear nor predictable in timing, and after a certain point, they are mutually ongoing forever. However, there is a tipping point, a critical mass threshold of sorts, where the overhaul of healing (i.e., cleaning the system of entangling nexus-knots, samskaras, and wounds) gives way to the spaciousness of liberation (i.e., what's left, or who you are in your natural state, as a result). This then becomes the point-of-no-return basecamp, a solid foundation on which to build.

Hold these concepts—*healing* and *liberation*—loosely, and what I have to say about them. What's important is to know that both are important, and indeed interrelated, but not the same thing. *True liberation cannot happen without healing of the past, and healing of the past does not automatically produce the liberation that I am pointing to in this book.* All parts must be incorporated, and all Five Basics engaged and practiced. All authentic interior paths have a transcendent, evolutionary component that is not found in the offices of mere psychoanalysts or psychologists or now-popular "life coaches." These places can be places of healing, but not always of liberation.

In fact, the healing arts have a major role to play in, and contribution to make to, our upgraded, sensitive-to-the-times-while-honoring-the-ancient interior systems. I am a "healing artist" myself with lots of training in the field. What I see as a shortcoming, from my experience and observation, is that we often approach the Eastern, "alternative" modalities with the same mindset as our fractured Western medical model. You'll hear many say, and I would agree, that when you snap your femur bone on a ski slope, don't go for an acupuncture treatment or herbal tea—you should get your ass to the hospital. The precise point is to *fix what's broken.* Exactly. But then back to the yoga studio, back to the bodyworker, back to the chiro for recovery and reintegration.

The problem, however, is that many of the Eastern methods now prominent in the West are adopted by *people*, and people do what people do—interpret everything based on their current lens, and take out of context an otherwise organic flowering of another culture. So not only do we use massage, energywork, Chinese medicine, yoga, etc. in a kind of buffet fashion (because we love our food buffets, so why not healing buffets, right?), but also in an attempt to kill the pain, suppress sensation, and fix something that's *wrong.* First point, what happens when you go to a buffet? You usually leave *stuffed* and feeling awful from *too much indulgence* (as well as from the mixing of all the ingredients). Second point, from my perspective, healing is about *wholling*; not fixing. It's about integrating the imbalance into regular, daily life experience; not about not feeling discomfort. Make sense?

So when I say the work on the interior helps to heal all past wounds, it doesn't mean all traces are automatically gone (though sometimes this may happen). When a tree gets struck by lightning, if it doesn't die, it simply keeps growing, now with a major burn mark that perhaps causes a branch to grow back twisted and gnarled. But so what? It may grow to be the tallest, most fruitful tree in all the forest, and is indeed "healed" from the traumatic damage, but it has that incident in its history and does not try to erase it. In fact, if the tree does continue to be healthy and strong, the strike and the affected bark become such small pieces of the entire ecosystem and experience of the whole life cycle, that in its transcendence, the little problems are now what Ken would call "distal" (meaning, further and further away from the current center of gravity of growth and being, and less and less defining that particular tree's identity).

Liberation, in the same way, is often fantasticized and romanticized into some unrealistic perfection in some faraway future. And lots of spiritual teachers and self-proclaimed gurus and enlightened masters don't help the matter. Liberation is both freedom *from* and freedom *in*, simultaneously, the world, the body, the mind, the personality, and all the shades of suffering, complexity, and existential contradiction this human enterprise brings. It's heart-wrenching and beautiful, and the proclamation by anyone that such a tension has been resolved once and for all is either lying or delusional or deceiving themselves and everyone else. When true healing and liberation happens, and "the Ultimates" are actuated in a real, organic, not airy-fairy way, the heart-wrenching part is no longer shunned, and the beautiful part is no longer clung to, and the heart-wrenching is seen to be beautiful, and the beautiful part heart-wrenching. There are points of no return, to be sure, and the higher-ups are indeed just that: higher up, richer, deeper, wider, more evolved, more profound...and yes, more beautiful, and yes, more heart-wrenching. Trust me and you will see.

In any case, the result of the work is well documented in all the traditions, but is usually misunderstood or even altogether unacknowledged. Remember the fruit of the Spirit? Remember Satcidananda? Remember tolerant, amused, kindhearted, dignified? These are qualities not to be *applied* in some sort of mechanical way, not to be repeated robotically while patterns and programs of the opposite are still beneath the surface running the show. No, they are what naturally happens, effortlessly, when and as you do the work. The work itself, or the Five Basics, is not something to *apply* to your life, but is rather a guiding principle or principles to *have a relationship with in your life*. And of course, to take the analogy further, just like the lightning-struck tree above, once fruit is produced, the plant does not stop growing (i.e., this is not some static end to the journey), but continues to produce more fruit as it grows and grows and grows!

So, along the way, ask yourself: Am I becoming, and seeing in myself and others, more or less of these fruits in my life? That, among other things, is the primary gauge of progress in my opinion. These fruits are not the relative, emotional, "feeling" versions of them, though this can happen as well; in other words, not possessive love (which is not love anyway), or conditional joy (like happiness when things go right), or a moment of peace in an otherwise chaotic world, or begrudging patience, or selfish kindness, not do-goodedness for reward or praise, not faithfulness to a belief system, not weak gentleness at the expense of standing strong, and not gripping, choking, white-knuckled self-control, not resentful or bitter tolerance, not dignified pride, not shallow and surface-level bliss... These fruits, in the more "Ultimate" sense, are abiding Presences and qualities of Being Itself, that indeed express through the personality, through the finite self, through feelings, into the exterior experience; but are first and foremost essential textures of the fabric of true humanity.

Welcome to the journey of all your lifetimes, the wildest ride you've ever ridden, and the most rewarding work anyone can do. I'm here to help you make it, so let us continue together, onto the first Basic.

Meditation Practice

———◆———

If you took a random poll asking the question *What is meditation?* you would get as many answers, if not more, as the number of people you asked. If you asked the same group of people *Why should someone meditate?* you could expect the same, with answers like, To calm the mind, To be less stressed, or even, Who says anyone should? If you asked ten self-proclaimed meditators *how* to meditate, again, more different answers, which may even include new meditative technologies like binaural beats or listening to guided meditations on podcasts. If you asked me to share *my* thoughts on the subject (which broadly is what this book is about, specifically this chapter), and compare my perspective with the hypothetical ones above, I would probably say that none of them are wrong, but that I'd like to take it a step or few further.

Why Meditate?

As I've already said, meditation is more than the technique, and is more than the twenty or thirty minutes set aside to practice. Meditation proper, or "the technique" (which is what we are discussing in this chapter) is and has always been a central and unavoidable component of all interior traditions. Not only does it provide a disciplined training of interior muscles (as I call them), and conscious awareness, or mindfulness, through all of the regular brainwave states that we pass through every twenty-four hours, but for me, the primary purpose of a meditation practice is to heal psycho-spiritual wounds and trauma, or *samskara* (which is the Sanskrit word from which we get our word "scar").

Any particularly traumatic or dramatic event, whether perceived as positive or negative, must be fully processed through all layers of the system (physical, energetic, emotional, mental, and spiritual). Any that are not create a nexus-knot of unresolved energetic entanglement. These nexus-knots drain the vitality of the overall "ecosystem" whether you know it or not, and will be the projection centers that repeatedly magnetize events in the exterior to re-inforce their existence on the interior (more on that in the Who Am I chapter).

The "layers of the system" themselves are also the same but different depending on the tradition. I like to use the Vedic model of the *koshas* (and *kosha* means precisely that—layer or sheath). In New Agey terms, this is known as the aura, and is becoming more than merely a woo-woo deception by palm readers that want to take your money. Scientific instruments are now able to detect and measure the existence, movement, and dysfunction of this energetic field (as well as the chakras, which we won't get into here). In any case, in the kosha system, there are five (the ones I already listed above)—physical or *anamayakosha*, energetic/emotional or *pranamayakosha*, mental or *manomayakosha*, intuitive/high-mental or *jnanamayakosha*, and spiritual or *anandamayakosha*. You will notice the word "maya" in each, which we will also cover in more detail in the Ultimates chapter. For now we can say that maya has come to be commonly translated as "illusion," but etymologically, it simply means "measurement." So, these are the measurements of the layers of the human energy field. And back to our point, any unresolved or not fully processed trauma or drama (no matter how major or minor) creates a correlate snag, tear, clog, or what I call a nexus-knot in one or all of these layers, and causes symptoms and manifestations, affecting in one way or other your life experience. It's a "blockage," preventing true vitality from flowing through.

Now, typically, our personality self, or *persona* (a word which in Latin means mask, and which we explore in more detail in the Who Am I? chapter), is the protective shell through which we interact with the world and others, and which, among other functions, serves to hide, protect, deny, ignore, or suppress the otherwise uncomfortable nexus-knots below the surface. The ones we'd rather not face, so the persona is our "best face forward" which refuses to look inward. Sometimes, if severe enough, the persona is fooling ourselves more than other people; pretending everything's okay when it's not, or pretending that the mask is who we really are, and that there's "nothing to see here" beneath the surface. During meditation, however, if the personality (along with the gross thinking mind)[14] is successfully "put to sleep," (i.e., the standard operating system, modus operandi, or normal thinking self is not active), then all of the *samskara* are allowed to finally process fully through the system in a non-threatening environment.[15]

This by no means means that it happens all at once. That's why a regular practice is necessary. What it does mean is that, once you commit on a regular basis[16] you can expect intermittent bursts of emotion, heightened trigger sensitivity, energetic release, and sometimes what feels like physical illness but is really just lodged toxicity getting dumped into the bloodstream as the system purges and processes these bound-up balls of trauma and drama. So take care of yourself, but recondition your initial interpretation to be positive, trusting, and consider that it's likely part of the work.[17] These bursts could be quick, could last all day, could last a few days, or even a whole season of life, depending on the depth of the roots and the degree of conditioning, attachment, and identification with the specific pattern. The bursts could occur *during* meditation, or could also play out after.[18] For example, if one of your layers holds a samskara from a wound in which you were injured or abused by another person (whether physically, sexually, emotionally, psychologically, doesn't matter), and that nexus-knot has not been processed, but has remained dormant and suppressed due to fear of facing it, and has built up a considerable amount of the emotion anger, then as your meditation practice unfolds, and that knot of tension is allowed to loosen, along with the loosening will be released all of the emotions surrounding the event—in this case, probably anger, rage, sadness, violation, untrust. As these emotions are literally now moving through the physiological system, and therefore the bloodstream and the brain, you may be even more susceptible to being triggered around that theme. But don't worry, it won't last forever. So this calls for even more vigilance and implementation of the rest of the Basics in this book. If you project further, react, or don't have the perspective I'm now giving you, it could abort the process. Simply stay with it, know that it's a really good thing, and it will pass. And in the wake of the intensity, there will be a noticeable new clarity, lightness, and ease around that particular issue. It doesn't mean it's all over, but a subconscious wave has surfaced, crashed, and receded, and a step up to higher ground has been accomplished. So you journey on.

Meditation to me, therefore, as you can tell, is not only about "calming the mind." A calm mind may (and will) come as a by-product, but before the calm is reached, some cleaning out of the junk is necessary. Paradoxically, after a "successful" twenty minute sitting practice, there is typically a positive shift in consciousness toward relaxation, presence, and peace, even if there is intensity of thoughts of emotions or bursts of unresolved nexus-knots. Though every teacher teaches meditation differently, and though it has become popular to simply listen to binaural beats or podcasts or guided meditation with the goal of calming the mind, I believe that some teachers do not provide the necessary support for students to let them know that when the "persona" is put to sleep, that's when all the buried stuff comes to the surface to be seen, felt, and processed.

A good mnemonic to remember it is: you have to *peel* back the layers, *reveal* what's underneath, and *feel* it in order to *heal* it. And this cannot be avoided. These nexus-knots are draining your energy anyway, and the subpersonalities formed from them are causing much suffering. So they will either affect you that way, possibly causing physical illness and disease, or you can release them. No other options exist. Because many teachers do not understand this process, they do not equip their students with the tools and the contextual understanding and emotional/intellectual support to persist in the tough times. And people inevitably drop out, quit, give up.

Mindfulness

All authentic meditation traditions have as one of their goals for practitioners to aim for maintaining conscious awareness, or mindfulness, through all states of consciousness (waking, dreaming, deep sleep, and the Ultimates)[19]—or simply, to be "mindful" all of the time.

Mindfulness itself has become a popular term, and in my opinion, as with most things popular, has lost its intended depth and breadth. Typically, when we hear teachers, or regular folk for that matter, talking about mindfulness, there is a certain implied strained focus and bandwidth limited to only the physical visual exterior world. According to Ken Wilber (and I would agree), there is *at least* the interior and exterior of the individual and collective,[20] and as meditation is typically interested in the individual interior, which is enough for a few lifetimes, that's not all there is to be mindful of. But let's say we're not assuming the physical visual world is the only world in which (and of which) to be mindful; let's say it's the interior of the individual altogether.

For starters, remember the koshas (or layers of the field)? Each of these layers has an interior or *subjectively felt* component as well as an exterior or *objectively observed* component. So, exteriorly, I have my physical body that I can see, I have my energy body that *some* can see and that all can touch and that instruments are now being created to detect, I have my mental body which can be measured by EEG machines, and I have my spirit body (aka the astral body, depending on who you ask) which is the one that perhaps goes on to other incarnate lives, and the one they were trying to measure to see how much it weighed in one experiment, and so on.[21] Interiorly, on the other hand, which is what meditation is concerned with, is the *feeling* that each of these layers or koshas or measured bodies (and the spaces they inhabit) has for me; uniquely for me, the individual.

Here, we are concerned with the ability to *mindfully* tune into the *feeling* of the physical body (and the corresponding gross, waking world), the *feeling* of the energy body (and the corresponding subtle, dreaming world), the *feeling* of the mental body (and the corresponding mind field itself), the *feeling* of the spirit body (and the corresponding deep, dreamless, causal world), and the *feeling* of Oneness (and the corresponding Ultimates Aware *of*, *as*, *with*, and *in* the Always-Already). As you can see, mindfulness is not a forced focus on chopping an onion or washing a dish or a strained and difficult introspection toward one's thoughts; it is a relaxed attention on any thing in any dimension (which could include but is not limited to mundane daily chores). The problem is, most people don't realize they can *train* this attention,[22] as well as broaden the bandwidth of the dimensions possible *for* attention! Most people are confined to the exterior visual physical world as real, and even if they have an experience of an "other" world or of an interior world, it's at best secondarily real, because they can't see[23] it physically; and it will be categorized (in their mind as well as how they talk about it) as such.

Brain Waves

From my perspective, mindfulness is the ability, as well as practiced, habituated skill, to be attentive to any thing at any time in any domain. In this regard, let's talk about states of consciousness in terms of brain waves, the interactive world they enact, and mindfulness in each. Remember, brain waves are objective, exterior correlates (which themselves have no meaning or feeling as such) of subjective, interior experiences. It is not so important that you understand or memorize the brain wave names (though it's really not so hard). What's important as far as I'm concerned is that you know it's a spectrum[24] that humans cycle through every twenty-four hours naturally; and meditatively, it is the same spectrum, but the invitation is to not "lose consciousness" like we are conditioned to do when our head hits the pillow at night.[25]

<u>Beta</u> In so-called "normal waking consciousness," when the active, linear, analytical, thinking self is operating, the brain is making *Beta*

waves. Mind-*less*-ness in this state is what I call "idle, autopilot mode," where basically the patterned fears and anxiety and stories and past/future torture and analytical, interpretive thinking are running the show, and "you" have "lost consciousness" while physically awake. Mind-*ful*-ness in this state can be practiced throughout the day as well as during a formal seated meditation: relaxed, attentive awareness of breathing, of bird sounds, of sensations in the body, of driving,[26] of communicating with another person, of the light in the room, of a candle flame, of drinking tea, or of a flower.[27] So, contrary to some opinions, normal waking consciousness is not *bad*, and contrary to other opinions, it is not the only realm to be mindful in and of.

Alpha There is an in-between state between normal waking (*Beta*), and dreaming (*Theta*)—it's called *Alpha*. Alpha can happen in a few ways: 1) in what some call a flow state, 2) on the cushion as hypnagogia, and 3) hypnagogia when "falling" asleep. We'll take these each briefly in turn.

The flow state is an easeful, expanded cooperation of mind and body during a (typically enjoyable) activity. Commonly reported is losing track of time, losing oneself in the moment, fluidity, and even periodic peaks in performance if it's a skill that can be judged by proficiency. A few examples of when the flow state is accessible are while doing yoga, gardening, painting, going for walks, and even playing sports.[28] I often experience it while writing.

Hypnagogia is a term referring to phenomena, typically in the form of images or sounds, but could be any of the senses, that warp or defy standard waking sensory input, and yet is clearly not a full-fledged dream. Everyone has had the experience, toward the beginning of the night, soon after your head hits the pillow and your system has shifted gears into sleep mode, of flashes of people's faces, quick sounds of voices or laughter, or a noted change in bodily sensation or spatial perception. Sometimes there is a feeling of falling (hence *falling* asleep), followed by jerking awake or a gasp for air. You know you weren't awake, and you know you weren't quite asleep. Those who claim ease in astral travel or can consciously induce out of body exploration say this is the window to access it. On the meditation cushion, for me, it's simply a helpful indication that I've moved into a different realm (i.e. have successfully implemented my chosen technique)[29] and am on my way to the deeper waters of *Theta* and *Delta*—I don't linger in hypnagogia-land; I simply keep it moving to what I consider the "good stuff."[30]

Before we get to *Theta*, I'd like to describe a couple of phenomena that happen regularly for me in some kind of medial realm between *Alpha* and *Theta*. It's as though, behind my closed eyelids, I can "see"—not physically optical, and not dream vision either—what some call the grid, and what some call wormholes. It's nothing in particular I do to "get there," but it often simply appears. The grid is basically just that: a sort of dual technicolor checker board extending into endless space. Usually there are two horizontal planes of the grid, one as a ceiling above, and one as a floor below, my vantage point—and they are moving quickly past me, or I am moving quickly into the Omega point on the horizon where they paradoxically never meet. Wormholes are in the same interior landscape space, but is literally like a tube or a tunnel that is moving past me, or that I am moving through, in up-and-down and round-and-round direction at lightning speed. The wormhole phenomenon is also likely to occur if something startles me awake at night just after falling asleep.

<u>Theta</u> In the dream state, the brain waves are in *Theta*. Typically, for normal sleepers, consciousness (in the relative sense) is lost, and we have to recall or remember the next morning what we dreamed. Again, some claim to maintain awareness during this, and to be able to participate as a body-mind-persona in their dreams just as they participate while awake. Here a distinction is important between the waking state being the "real world" and it simply being another realm with another body and another self. The paradox is that they are all unmistakably experienced as *you* (or, "I," because I Am-ness never leaves), but remember from the kosha conversation, that you have more than just a physical body, and these very bodies are your vehicles to operate in many different realms. My opinion is that we are simply not trained to activate these, or to register the other realms as real; we shouldn't confuse this lack of training and blindspots as "not real." In fact, many traditions hold the meditative and dream realms

to be more real than the waking.

In any case, we come back to normal waking consciousness in the morning and remember our dreams. And the dreams were dreamed as a self-reflexive "I," hence the standard, "Last night I dreamed I was [whatever it was]." Notice there are at least three selves in this sentence (the grammar gives it away): There is the I who dreamed, the I in the dream, and the I that *must have been aware* of the dream in order to be able to remember the dream in the morning! Of course there has been lots of research done, and there is a rich history of dream interpretation and why we dream what we dream (dating all the way back to Biblical times and before, and Jungian analysis in present day), and I am not an expert in that particular field; but suffice it to say, it's a *whole world unto itself* that you can stabilize and be consciously attentive in, and interactive with...either in bed, on the cushion, or both![31]

On the cushion, when the brain is producing *Theta* waves (in what Ken Wilber calls the subtle state or realm), it is similar to the experience of night time dreams, but the meditator is fully conscious. For me, it's not so much that full story lines play out—then again, that's not really how I dream anyway—but that the hypnagogic experiences from *Alpha* simply become more pronounced, detailed, and vivid (after all, it's just a quick turn of the dial to the next channel over). There can be flashes of people's faces that are clear and distinct, right in front of me staring back, that I've never seen before. Occasionally I also have loud crackling pops that undoubtedly originate somewhere in my skull and not as a dream, and definitely not "outside" in the environment. I've been told this is either the pineal gland activating or what Barbara Brennan calls the Hara Line connecting to its Omega point above the head in another dimension.

In my opinion, this state is just as elusive and under-understood as the dream state during the night; i.e., where do these *really* come from? What's going on, where am I going, who am I seeing? Standard dreams, besides the possibility of being archetypal communication, are more of a "sorting" or "organizing" or "making sense" of all the subconscious, not-yet-processed fragments of thoughts and experiences from the previous day or so. Usually, you know where the bits and pieces come from, even if they are jumbled and mashed together in a strange way. On the cushion, however, for me, there is rarely a reference to an "actual" happening in my exterior life, which leads me to believe that I am tuning in to another realm or a higher frequency of...myself? The Hologram? Who knows? Basically (in addition to dreamlike visions or hypnagogia), the *Theta* zone can utilize any of the senses from the waking world and "push" them into the subtle world, even mixing them together, thus bending their typical reception and expression in a kind of "trippy" way—and it gets even curiouser the more you are able to maintain a steady, relaxed focus (and hone the skill of mediation) for an extended period of time.

By way of example, here are a few memorable moments from my Theta *states:*

Example #1. When I first was learning to meditate, one of my first "successful" stabilizations in the subtle realm was one in which I "saw" behind closed eyelids a vast, black, velvety body of water. My entire field of "vision" (though again, it was not exterior, physical vision, but indeed was known to be some kind of "optical" input) was consumed with this deep, endless, darkness (interpreted as water). For the entire time of the meditation, I was able to maintain focus with a curious, amused detachment, while *observing* every *sound* making waves and ripples across the water in the *shape* of the tone itself (as I said, sometimes the senses even mix; there's no other way to describe it). Whenever someone in the room would cough, for example, the cough would make a sound wave signature across my vision field. When a car would drive by outside, the same thing would happen, mimicking and mirroring the speed, pace, vibration, and volume of the sound. My teacher used to test us by walking around the room, intentionally making noises, heavy steps, and dropping keys in order to challenge our focus. Everything he did also made a ripple across the water. This particular experience also invoked a particularly memorable "integration" period after the sitting and for the rest of the evening: When we "came back" and were sharing around the circle what we had experienced, I could hardly say with words, though I knew quite clearly the profoundness and clarity of what I had just heard-seen-felt. I simply sat in stillness and quietly asked if I could please have a pass. As I drove home, I felt a natural, though unusual, easeful sense of calm and presence the likes of which I didn't remember having had before. I had certainly tipped into another state of consciousness, and had done so *intentionally*, and that to me was fascinating and worth exploring further.

Example #2. Two other memorable, but depending on who you ask, rather disturbing, flashes occurred within only a couple of weeks of each other. One was of a man on an operating table with two people in lab coats and other surgical attire standing over him and buzzsawing his skull open. Yep, that. It wasn't maniacal or bloody or even scary; just sterile and matter-of-fact—this is what's happening, this is what I'm seeing. And though when I came back to the waking state I was a bit shocked and shaken ("What the...?"), during the meditation, it was quite neutrally observed, and I felt both removed and at the same time not needing to turn away or run. Quite engaged. Sort of like, "Huh...that's interesting." The point of view was from one of the ceiling corners of the room, looking down, which made me wonder if I wasn't, from my current meditation cushion, peering into another lifetime as my soul was leaving my body. I don't watch "scary" movies, I don't have violent thoughts or fantasies, and I don't remember any past references to a scene such as that that my brain could have been processing. As I said above, it wasn't a full-fledged dream or scenario with a storyline; but a clear pictorial flash that was more than merely hypnagogic.

The other semi-disturbing scene was—again, soon after the buzz-saw one, maybe a week later—of a man in dreadlocks locked up in the stocks...you know, the torture device from back in the day where the head goes through one hole and the hands go through the other holes on either side of the head. Again, no idea, except the possibility of a past life or clairvoyance of some kind, what exactly it was and why it showed up in meditation. These are well-worn grooves in uncharted and highly individualized territories. So your best guess is as good as mine, and as always, beware of anyone who claims to tell you they know *exactly* what any of this is and what it means.

Example #3. During one *Theta* experience I did in fact watch an entire scene play out. Again, watching from above, a woman was running to catch a cab in the rain, opened the door, swung her head around left and right as though looking for someone (or trying to avoid someone), her hair flying around as she did, got in the cab, and the cab drove off. Sounds sort of normal-ish, right? Maybe like a dream? Well, the thing is, it was in *cartoon!* Literally, the woman was a two-dimensional cartoon character, the raindrops were big, caricatured, overexaggerated drops, the cab was like a cardboard cutout, the movements were jerky, and the colors were slightly off from "real life" 3-D waking state colors—a little more neon (her hair was neon orange), the cab a brighter yellow, the atmosphere a moody gray, much like you might see in a comic book. Just as I don't watch scary movies, I don't watch cartoons either, and did not recognize any of this from any memories or references whatsoever. That, again, is a clue that it's *something else*—not a dream in the traditional sense. The other difference of course is that *Theta* experiences during meditation are in a fully conscious state, much like is reported of a lucid dream. During the above examples, and others similar that I have had, I am fully immersed in what I am observing, in the moment it's happening, fully aware that I am meditating, and fully certain that I am not making it up. Again, no other way to describe it.

Example #4. A couple more, just to give you an adequate idea of the flavor of this realm. The following is a regular occurrence for me. Some schools call it "mind awake, body asleep," and for me, it's often a little closer to the *Beta/Alpha* or *Alpha/Theta* transition point.[32] The felt experience is of the physical body becoming simultaneously almost nothing and at the same time immensely dense and heavy. If I have my fingers crossed, hands folded in my lap, for example, they will feel like a single thick clod of clay; or my crossed legs will feel like they are being swallowed in quicksand beneath me. But meanwhile, my mind is very clear, lucid, and arguably more "awake" than in the waking state. This has never been interpreted with panic or anxiety because of the calm, neutral presence witnessing it; but it may in some people, I don't know. For me it's extremely intriguing, and if I can maintain that level of mental focus, and not trip over further into deeper *Theta* or *Delta*, and if I don't come all the way back up for air so to speak (thus cycling back to the surface), I find it fun to mobilize my consciousness and explore all the strange sensations, visuals, and realms that the body/mind is experiencing there.

Example #5. Lastly, a common phenomenon, especially if I'm not resting my back in a chair but have my spine free-floating on a bolster or meditation cushion, and as I'm dropping deeper in, is that my spine and torso starts to sway, or even "fall" over to the right or the left, and I am entirely aware of it, but completely not in control of my body until a physiological signal is sent to the brain, "HE'S GONNA HIT THE FLOOR!" and then I catch myself and sit back up straight again. During the above cartoon example, for example, there was a more controlled version of this. My head, neck, and spine were floating straight up, balancing weightlessly, and as the cartoon began playing out, I began to very subtly and slowly lean to the right, my head tilting ever so slightly to the right, and was completely aware of it. I consciously held myself there, not letting the body fall, yet not bringing it all the way back up either, and there was the distinct feeling that the cartoon was happening "over there, down there," to the right and down, and that if I lifted back up, I would lose the scene.

There are countless varieties of experience possible in the *Theta* state, and still lots of research (in neuroscience as well as from practitioners' direct experience) to be done to determine and get a better understanding of the *what* and *why*, and how it's different from regular dream state during sleep. But for me, it's not only part of the path to healing and liberation, but also a quite entertaining side show (better than any series on TV).[33]

Delta The *Delta* state is also known as the Causal realm, and is the "deep dreamless sleep" that we enter into at least a couple of times every night. In this state, whether on the cushion or in the bed, the body is gone, the mind is gone, the personality is gone, the world is gone; no thoughts, no dreams, no past, no future, no ideas. Nothing. If one is not privy to what's happening here, or doesn't inquire into the highly subtle and profound mystery of such an Empty Void, it's very easily overlooked or just thought to be a blank blip-out during the night. But even so, where'd you go during the blank blip-out? Some don't even think about it; it's just, "I went to sleep, I had some dreams, and then I woke up." But if you inquire into the "who" that you mean when you say you went to sleep, you dreamed, and you woke up, and ask, "Who is this 'I' who did these things," then a deeper insight is realized; namely, that there not only was a steady stream of "I-ness" throughout all states, and now including the waking, but also that there was rather a *different* I or self that embodied or experienced each one[34]—is the waking I the same as the dreaming I the same as the dreamless I the same as the one remembering them now? There must have been an I, or a state of awareness, that was indeed aware for you to be able to wake up and remember what you dreamed and also remember the blank blip-out when there was nothing arising. You simply lost "attention" or consciousness (relatively).

But in meditation, if you can maintain a steady, relaxed focus long enough, and move through and beyond the subtle space of images and hypnagogia, there is an undeniable experience of this Causal realm. It's my favorite place. The way I experience it, and a pretty accurate way that I have found to describe it, is *Pure Presence Aware of Nothing*. If you've never been there consciously, what I am about to say won't mean much; but just tuck it away for when it does happen (or imagine what it might be like, as a sort of morphic field that pulls you up): Nothing itself can become something, and in a way, the Causal realm *is* a sort of space of nothingness (and thus a something called nothing) that I am aware of. Simple as that. Notice, as we've said, there is an "I" that is aware of each different state or realm or dimension or space inhabited. It may be the Pure Witness, or it may be the finite self (and if it is the finite self, then the Pure Witness is also aware of that, aware of the Causal realm). Again, if you've never experienced this in meditation, just think of being "awake" during deep dreamless sleep, and you got it cognitively, and that's something to aim for.

If, during meditation, you think from time to time you "fell asleep," or "blanked out," without images or dreams, chances are you actually went to the Causal realm, but the "consciousness" or "attentiveness" muscle has not been awakened or is not yet strong enough to "remember" it, or to be aware of it when it's happening. That's why this is a practice, and takes time. But allow my words and descriptions to carry you along, priming the pump intellectually until you eventually "see" it for yourself. I read and read and read and intellectualized and conceptualized these concepts for years before I finally got it directly. That doesn't mean it will take years for you too; just know that the concept is not the same as the experience (or as Ken Wilber says, the map is not the same as the terrain); but both are irreconcilably important.

It's like planning a trip to a remote jungle that you have heard stories of but have never been to yourself. In preparation, you watch documentaries, look at photos, and talk to other people who have been; you have developed a "sense" of what it's like, but you still don't know first-hand (you're still projecting and comparing from your current perspective); you have an image in your mind and even a feeling of being there, of what you might do there, or how you might like it, but you don't have any past references to go on. You might look at a map, plan your adventures, and have some intentions of possible activities. But it's not until you arrive that you have the undeniable experience of *Ooohhh! That's what they were talking about!*...and are now able to contextualize and integrate the planning and projecting with the real thing to make it now your own. It's not so different in meditation. Some sources or teachers or authors or traditions may provide the framework, and others may blow you over the edge...and, what's more, this can happen with all of the Five Basics (by which I mean a cognitive vs. experiential dichotomy and relationship).

So back to our point. The reason it's called the Causal realm is because everyone who has ever consciously been there comes back with the same interpretation, or some variation on it—namely, *Whoa, it seems like the entire world arises from this place and falls back into it.* Therefore, this is what "causes" everything (at least from the direct, phenomenological viewpoint; we still of course don't know the answer to the age-old question, *Well what caused that?* God. *Well who made God?* Or even, *It all evolved from a single-celled organism* begs the obvious chain of inquiry, *Where did that come from?* Spontaneous, random collision in a primordial stew. *Well who or what cooked the stew?* And on and on and on. In both first-person as well as third-person perspectives, we've never figured it out, never gotten behind the Curtain. The universe gets bigger every time we try to find the edge, and smaller every time we try to find the smallest part. From an ultimate perspective, there is no end to Awareness Itself.[35] And of course, this is still speaking in the realm of dualistic, cause-and-effect, even if a very deep understanding of it. It seems pretty clear, even if you have not consciously experienced the Causal realm (and see if you can confirm this with at least a tentative Yes even now...), that upon falling asleep at night, when the gross, physical world vanishes, it dissolves into the more subtle, dreamtime world, which then vanishes into pure nothingness, and then dreams emerge again from there, followed by the waking world emerging from the dreamtime world. All in a cycle. Yes? *Where did the world go? From whence did it return?* and *Who was there to watch it?* So the Causal realm is sort of a Void (the Emptiness of emptiness), or a black hole at the center of your being. And you do experience it every single night.[36]

Hear an excerpt from the Tao Te Ching 16:[37]

Empty your mind of all thoughts
Let your heart be at peace
Watch the [rise and fall] of beings
But contemplate their return
Each separate being in the universe returns to the common source
Returning to the source is serenity

During meditation, as the conscious mind is more attentive, you can slow down the experience of the *Delta* wave Causal realm rather than crashing into it and being spit back out of it so mindlessly. As you do, you'll notice a few characteristics. There is a sense of being, what I like to call, "wide aware"—an undoubtable sense that You Are. However, there is no body, no chair, no meditation cushion, not even breathing. Your physical eyes may be closed, but there is a clarity of "seeing" into the infinite nothingness;[38] it's a rich, velvet blacker-than-black. If you've been there, you know; and if you haven't and it sounds scary, it's only scary to the ego, whose job is to keep itself alive, and who is nowhere to be found in the Causal realm—so no wonder! Rather than a feeling of true absence or lack, there is a very immanent and intimate Presence, closeness, Hereness. If there is absence, it's simply an absence of suffering, of cause and effect in the physical realm, an absence of thinking, an absence of all little-me's. And That Which is left after they are gone is unforgettable. Sometimes, as the attention muscle is strengthened, there can be a fuzzy (but clear) sort of way-in-the-background thought that goes something like, "I...am...here...," but there are no thoughts *about* anything; again, no-thing at all. The head may be the dropped, but you are not even aware of this, because there is no time and no space in this place; you are only aware that the head *was* dropped when you "come out" of it into *Theta*, *Alpha*, or *Beta* and you have to lift your head. Again, the head could be down, and the eyes closed, but the sensation (if you can even call it that) is of looking straight ahead into an endless abyss.

Another characteristic of *Delta* is that you may also notice sacred geometrical shapes (or vague archetypal images) coming and going within the Nothing. If you are unfamiliar with sacred geometry, I would highly recommend at least a beginner's understanding of it.[39] In a nutshell, sacred geometry is the geometric (and, vicariously, mathematic) representation of the most basic constituent parts that the manifest world is made up of. Therefore, wouldn't it make sense that, if you can maintain focus, you would see these forms taking shape in the Causal realm before the manifest world comes fully back? Often I see the flower of life, or a swirling pupil and eyeball; this is where the archetypes live, and they are directly understood to be not a dream and not from the thinking, imaginative mind.[40]

A brief note regarding the Causal realm as it relates to the Ultimates. It was here that I began directly tuning into the Ultimate Witness or I Am Presence due to the unmistakable *Awareness aware of nothing* perception. This same Pure Awareness is also the one aware of all somethings in the waking and dreaming worlds; but because those worlds are so crowded and populated with *things*, it's easier to miss That Which Is Aware *of* the things. In the Causal, it's impossible to miss.

Brain Wave (& Sleep & Meditation) Summary

Frederick Buechner, my favorite of all time writer, sums up the normal cycle in beautiful poetic prose:

> You wake up out of the huge crevasses of the night and your dreaming. You get out of bed, wash and dress, eat breakfast, say goodbye and go away never maybe to return for all you know, to work, talk, lust, pray, dawdle and do, and at the end of the day, if your luck holds, you come home again, home again. Then night again. Bed. The little death of sleep, sleep of death. Morning, afternoon, evening—the hours of the day, of any day, of your day and my day...
>
> "In the beginning God created the heavens and the earth. The earth was without form and void, and darkness was upon the face of the deep; and the Spirit of God was moving over the face of the waters. And God said, 'Let there be light.'" Creation *ex nihilo*. Light out of darkness; Order out of chaos; Waking out of sleep.
>
> The furnace is turned down and the window open a crack. The shoes are side by side near the window, their toes slippery with moonlight and emptiness where flesh and blood

belong. The five-year diary is more than four years full... The darkness falls on the just and the unjust, the hero and the pig, the quick, the quicker, and the not so quick. The shoes are my cousins, the table my aunt, the tock of the wicker rocker livelier than my ticker. I do not own these things; we are all things together. I do not have a body; I am a body.[41] And darkness is upon the face of my face...

The chaos of sleep, the *tohu wabbohu*[42] of dreams. If our waking world, the world of Ten Thousand Things, is threatened by a population explosion, only consider the problem as it exists in the world of dreams where there are not only all the living to domicile but all the dead too not to mention the others, all the might-have-beens and the might-be-yets, the world of Ten Thousand times Ten Thousand Things and un-Things...

Beneath the moonlit drifts of sheet, I turn in my sleep and draw up my knees except that there is no *I* at this moment but just my knees which draw up themselves by some complex autonomy of bones, tendons, muscles, like an empty self-service elevator working off calls from floor to floor after closing time...

Darkness was upon the face of the deep, and God said, "Let there be light." Darkness laps at my sleeping face like a tide, and God says, "Let there be Buechner." Why not? Out of the primeval chaos of sleep he calls me to be a life again. Out of the labyrinth of selves, born and unborn, remembered and forgotten, he calls me to be a self again, a single true and whole self. He calls me to be this rather than that; he calls me to be here rather than there; he calls me to be now rather than then. He calls me to be of all things me as this morning when the alarm went off or the children came in or your dream woke you, he called you to be of all things you. To wake up is to be given back your life again. To wake up—and I suspect that you have a choice always, to wake or not to wake—is to be given back the world again and of all possible worlds this world, this earth rich with the bodies of the dead as our dreams are rich with their ghosts, this earth that we have seen hanging in space, our toy, our tomb, our precious jewel, our hope and our despair and our heart's delight. Waking into the new day, we are all of us Adam on the morning of creation, and the world is ours to name. Out of many fragments we are called to put back together a self again.[43]

To conclude, if these are the typical brain wave states and patterns that we go through every twenty-four hours, and are also what's possible to experience consciously in meditation, then the question becomes, "Who is it that's aware of all of this?" Who, in fact, is the constant, steady I that contains the changes, and remembers that there was no *I* when the knees bent up in bed? Who is the I that maintains awareness to remember that part of you lost consciousness? Who is the one that must have been there for you to be able to wake up in the morning and say, "Oh yes, I slept good last night," or to be able to even know what I mean, and have at least a hazy memory of something called deep dreamless sleep, that part of the night, just last night, you know, when everything, even your sense of self, went away? Who is it? Who but you? Who but the same I that has been looking through your eyes through all the years of birthdays and all the way back to your birth day? The same one unchanging and unchanged through all the wavering waves of life and all the dreams of night and day. Has it changed? Have you? Or have you always been...Always Only I...?

Technique

Briefly, I should say that currently, I am only recommending, for technique(s) to practice, the guided meditations on the homepage of my website, kgraykaliana.com—The Unnamed Kaliana Meditation Method, Be Present With What Is, and Phase 3. There are sure to be more, but the only way that I know how to assess and assist your progress is for you to stay within the suggestions of the Kaliana Container (a further description of what I mean by this is also on the homepage). There are ample options to choose from and work with within the given techniques, and they all collectively include characteristics of many others I have learned and been trained in. At the same time, no one has ever explicitly taught them to me —they are somewhere between inspired, downloaded, channeled, and made-up or discovered in my own experimentation! Please do not use the guidance every time, but use it for support, and eventually learn how to do them on your own. Also recommended is to find a rhythm, routine, schedule, and frequency that works for you; it helps to have at least some consistency, at least at the beginning, so that your system responds to the coming shift in a similar way as it responds when you lie down in bed at night. 20-30 minutes per day is ideal, more is great, and shorter is fine if that's all the time you have. A lot more can be said about the nuts and bolts and logistics of a meditation practice, but I won't take up more space here for that. Reach out directly (through my website) if you have questions or need further clarification or coaching specific to your unique situation.

The Ultimates

———— • ————

In addition to a regular meditation practice, it is important to attune your awareness to what I call "the Ultimates." Some teachers teach that after waking, dreaming, and deep sleep, there are only two more "states" of consciousness (that are not really states at all, because states by nature come and go and these do not, but are ultimate realizations that, when you look, are "always already" there).[44] These are typically called the Witness and the Nondual perspective (which, again, is not really a perspective...). However, in my direct experience, study, and understanding, these are only two of many Ultimate states.[45] In Patanjali's *Yoga Sutras*, for example, there are multiple words used to describe the Ultimate state of Samadhi: *savichara samadhi, nirvichara samadhi, savitarka samadhi,* and *nirvikalpa samadhi* to name only a few. The word Samadhi itself connotes something like "Oneness."[46] I am not a Sanskrit or *Yoga Sutras* scholar, and I do not want to impose my Western conditioned opinion on what exactly Patanjali meant, and what exactly is experienced by those who have been raised in traditional Yoga cultures, so I will not attempt to draw precise parallels between their terms and mine.[47] The Buddhist tradition has a similar litany of Ultimates. That's because, all who have dared to dive deeply and look (including myself) have come up with the same experience of multiple "flavors" of Ultimate states.

For the casual explorer, they may all be lumped into two generic categories, as mentioned, commonly referred to as Witness and Nondual, in the same way as a non-connoisseur of wine just knows the difference between red and white, sweet and dry; or a non-connoisseur of coffee just knows dark or light, robust or mild. But the connoisseur knows the notes and the palate and where and how the beans or the grapes were grown and can dissect the entire experience from vine to pour to tongue. Suffice it to say I am a connoisseur of these Ultimate states. The one common strand amongst them (in the same way as the common strand amongst the various flavors of coffee is the coffee bean itself, and the common strand amongst the various wines is the grape itself) is that they are universally always already the case. The only time it seems otherwise is when the ego has confiscated the finite self and has turned its attention away from That Which Is, or clouds have come in front of and eclipsed the sun and the identity is on the ground side of the clouds. We go deeper into this in the Who Am I? chapter. For now, let's continue hammering home the Ultimates, with the help of an inevitable explanation of what is *not* Ultimate.

Ultimate vs Relative

To reiterate, in a more cohesive fashion, the difference between ultimate and relative as philosophical concepts in general apply to anything I say. Put very succinctly, *Ultimate means it does not change, relative means it changes.*[48] And in my approach, there are ultimate and relative "versions" of most of the states of being and consciousness that we explore.

Relatives know themselves only in comparison to what they are not. The only thing the Ultimate is *not* is relative,[49] but that does not mean it knows itself that way—it simply knows itself itself, and you can know it (and know yourself as That) in a self-confirming way just by looking, too. The relative operates on spectrums in the phenomenal world. As we said in the Meditation chapter, please do not automatically interpret "phenomenal" to mean the visual, exterior, physical realm only, which is what we typically preference as the "real world." If it's a phenomenon, that means it *happens*, and that you can *experience* it. So, sound happens, light happens, feelings happen, thoughts happen, out-of-body experience happens, birth happens, death happens, soul travel and meetings with otherworldly beings happen, taste happens, anger happens, the Causal Nothing as a something happens, rain happens, flowers happen, tragedy happens, God happens, enlightenment happens.[50] These are all still relatives, albeit on multiple *levels* and *layers* and *densities*, degrees and spectrums nonetheless.

Another characteristic of relatives is that they are infinite and eternal *in* time and space (Ultimates, on the other hand, operate *as* Infinity and Eternity itself, *beyond* time and space).[51] Remember also that time and space, we are discovering, are themselves not fixed, but relative and malleable constructs that simply appear dense and constant in our dimension. Relatives also have a way of approaching the Ultimate, while still staying on the relative "side of the street" (to use a Ken Wilber phrase). For example, I remember in high school Geometry class, we did a thought experiment in which the teacher stood a certain distance away from the wall and said, "If I move half the distance closer to the wall, will I reach the wall?" to which of course we all rolled our eyes, "Duh, No!" So she moved to that approximate distance, halfway to the wall, and then she asked it again: "How about now? If I move half the distance closer to the wall, will I reach the wall?" Scratching our heads, and not yet understanding the mind-blow that was coming (at least for me), yet again, "Come on lady, what's the point? No!" So she moved half the distance closer. On the next time, because she, as a human-size body, was getting "relatively" (get it?) pretty close to the wall, I jumped ahead to the conclusion before she even asked the question and realized, "Holy Mother of Measurement! If she continues like that, she'll never ever never ever never ever in time or space reach the wall!" All the way down to the most infinitesimal decimal point! That was a considerably profound cognitive awakening that I had in my high school math class that has stayed with me to this day and which I apply to many considerations in meditation, spirituality, and philosophy. I'm sure there's a smarty-pants way of saying this mathematically, but let's just say the relative, in its endlessness, can come *close* to an Ultimate, but itself *never reaches it!* It cannot and will not, ever! The Ultimate is "something else" altogether, and yet, again, paradoxically, is what allows the relative to be in the first place, and is not known by us phenomenal creatures without knowing a relative. The Ultimate knows itself as itself, and is known by us because it's the first and only thing we've seen or experienced consciously that's *not* known by what it's not. Whoa. Mind. Blown. Yeah?

This is why, in my view (and again, probably someone else has already said this in their own scientifically formulated format, but I'll put it in my own words from my experience here), there are *no such things as opposites*. If each spectrum of perception, whether it be light or sound or sensation or density of thought or anything whatsoever that can be perceived in time and/or space, in and of itself is relative, but is itself endless in both directions, then where oh where would opposites lie? I believe that this is a clear representation of a higher level of cognition in general, that correlates with our new understanding of the "material world." For example, in lower levels, when we believed the Earth to be the center of all created things, and that it was flat (don't get me started about the Flat Earth Theory of today), and that heaven was "up" and that hell was "down," there were easy peasy references to this vs that, up vs down, here vs there, now vs then, white vs black, hot vs cold, happy vs sad (and this is of course a necessary but very toddlerish way to think). Now, we know the universe, or multiverse (whatever these things even are, computer simulations, holograms, higher order video games in which *we* are being played...?), is expanding in "all directions, all dimensions" *endlessly* (sound familiar?). And of course our planet is spherical which means "up" has no meaning anymore! How about down? Left? Right? Think about it... *Think* about it! In any case, the best we can do is make comparisons from one relative to another. There are no opposites. There can be poles relating with each other, there can be fulcrums along the way within this little segment and this little segment and this little bandwidth and this little octave, but not truly opposites the way we were taught opposites in hellementary school.

Let's slow it down for a moment. Chew and digest if you need to. If you're getting overwhelmed, stop, meditate, journal, re-read what you just read. Just letting these words and concepts light up in your awareness kickstarts an automatic psycho-spiritual awakening. There is no rush.

The Ultimate is that-which-always-already-is, of whatever flavor. Remember, there are many different Samadhis. Many different Ultimates to taste-test. And in your exploration, the litmus question is *does it have a beginning and end in time and space?* If yes, it's relative. If no, it's Ultimate. *Is it always-already Itself, unchanging* (besides the paradoxical "change" in the experience *of* it)? If yes, it's Ultimate. If it changes (whether theoretically, potentially, or actually), it's relative. In the Who Am I? chapter, we go further into relative vs ultimate *identity.*[52] For now, suffice it to say in general (and this is a good mantra to remember), *If it has a beginning and an end in time and space, it is relative. If not, it is Ultimate.*[53] Or, *If it is always-already the case, it's Ultimate.*

But why does this matter? (And I would invite you again and again to return to this question as we go along: So what?) How does this fit into the overall picture here of interior survival and thrival? How does this integrate with my life and practice, rather than just taking Kemper's word for it? To me, this matters, the difference between relative (any thing) and Ultimate (any flavor), because on a practical level, and back to Spirituality 101, any "ultimate" attachment to, identity with, or reliance for happiness on, some thing in the phenomenal, relative world will cause suffering, period. Either when that thing changes and you're not ready for it to change, when it goes away and you want to keep it, when it won't go away and you want it to...or simply in the inevitable manipulatory relationship you develop in *trying* to get it to change, stay, go away, or be a certain way. The only suffering possible with regard to the Ultimate is pretending you are not already that. Hafiz says, "My separation from God is the most difficult thing in the world."[54] And Jesus says, in *A Course In Miracles* (and I'm paraphrasing this one), *Arrogance is not believing you are God; arrogance is believing you are not.*

Within the Ultimate, as the Ultimate, there is no suffering. All is already given. Nothing is needed. No clinching, no clinging, no contraction. You are always-already beyond time. You are always-already free. You are always-already whole. You are always-already content, peaceful, joyous. You are always-already Home. If there is any discomfort or rebuttal or "yeah-but" here, it's only from the ego who wants to hold onto that which it can't (and never has been able to) hold onto in the first place. On a deeper level, you already know who you are. You already know the truth of what I'm saying. You only have to give up that which you are not; and isn't just the thought of that liberating?

I am never claiming a cold, dead, lifeless spirituality; quite the contrary, as are all authentic spiritual traditions. You just have to have the eyes to see what we're saying. It's a repurposing of priority, identity, and center of gravity. Jesus says (this time in the good ole Bible), "Seek first [the] Kingdom...and *all these things will be yours as well*."[55] What else could that mean? Before you understand this reprioritization, hold lightly *relative things*, and once the shift has occurred, then you will understand, and the ones that are supposed to come back will come back; the ones that are not, won't, and you probably didn't want them to begin with anyway. Then the world will be imbued with the light of divine consciousness, clear seeing, and beauty beyond any sting of death. This is the true meaning of, "O death, where is your victory? O death, where is your sting?"[56] In other words, the *clinging to things was causing the sting*. And remember, relative "things" are not just "worldly possessions" in the physical sense (though of course it includes that as well), but are also ideologies held too tightly, belief systems, any role as a personality or career, status, money, fame, expectations or agendas about the future, the need to be right, the need to protect, the need to succeed, the fear of failure, or any aggrandized need whatsoever. The list goes on and on, yes, endlessly on, along the whole spectrum of relativity. *Anything that was given, can be taken away,* and thus is included in this list. *Anything that can change* is included in this list. *Anything that is not always-already* is included in this list. Any. Thing.

The other reason that this is important (again, continuing to circle back to the question So what?) is because if the distinction between relative and Ultimate is not understood at the outset of this interior journey, as you do your work and remember and implement The Basics (one of which is this very chapter: return to the Ultimates regularly), then you will sell yourself short, and have a very cut-off experience of the Ultimate. The Ultimate is the Ultimate is the Ultimate, and if it is not, it will be an undercooked experience (and will be, across the board, no questions, *only relative*, and a misconstrued realization and claim of something it isn't) and will potentially disappoint or eventually cause suffering, because it will become just another "thing" to cling to (and potentially lose), yet again.

What's more, if the ego is not dismantled, but is in fact the one directing the show to make sure you *do not* truly see the Ultimate but merely a high-vibe, entertaining and perhaps pretty version of the relative, then the seeing is not true and the Ultimate still left lingering out of reach. It is enticing to preference one of these relative experiences (and stop short) because of the feel-good, comfortable, familiar reference of relativity, and it is enticing, if the Ultimate is glimpsed, to confiscate it and make it a "thing." But then of course it immediately ceases to be the Ultimate. Any thought of the Ultimate is still just a thought (coming and going); any idea of the Ultimate, the same. Even (and this gets a little terminologically tricky) any experience of the Ultimate is just another experience. Let that sink in. *Any experience of the Ultimate is just another experience.*

That's why all authentic spiritual, meditative, esoteric, interior traditions, particularly the ones with a lineage holder or guru figure or master of sorts, took very seriously that students and practitioners get the true download (the shakti pot) and not a filtered-through watered-down shallow swing-and-a-miss. It wasn't a control mechanism. It was a desire to ensure that the purity of the seeing lives on and is passed down appropriately and is not skewed. It can be easily side-swiped. So students would spend many many sessions with the teacher describing their realizations and being confirmed that yes, you are seeing correctly, or being challenged to go back to the cushion and keep practicing. A very enlightened-sounding response needs to be tested and questioned before automatically confirming, *Yes! You got it!* The flash of insight (Satori in Zen) also must take root and begin producing fruit. Sound familiar? The fruit of the Spirit. And again, By their fruits you will know them.[57] How is it spilling over into your life? How is it infusing itself into your exterior world? How is it changing your patterns and programs of suffering? Are you becoming happier, more peaceful, more joyful, more loving, more selfless? Are you holding the relative world more lightly, and at the same time with more care and intention, seeing its perfection and beauty as it was meant to be? Then you're making progress! Keep it up!

Maya & Illusion

You may have heard the Sanskrit word *maya*, and if you've been in the pop-spiritual-culture world for a while, you may have heard that "maya means illusion." But, in standard Kemper fashion, I'd like to break this whole thing apart. Do you even know what illusion means? What *you* mean by illusion? Do you take it for granted? Does illusion mean "not real?" Have you ever tried to reconcile the frustrating contradiction that goes something like, *If all of this is an illusion, why does it seem so real? Or How could I be staring right at something that doesn't exist?* That, in my opinion, is a misunderstanding of what "real" and "illusion" means in the first place. Etymologically, *maya* doesn't mean "illusion." Firstly, it means *measurement*. Ah! Now we're getting somewhere. So, as with all words, in their original purpose, whoever first used the word maya to refer to something like illusion knew what they were saying, just like the first person who used the word *persona* to mean personality knew what they were saying (which we get to in the Who Am I? chapter). What they were pointing to was the truth that anything with measurement (therefore any thing, any phenomenon, any relative, in any dimension or domain) is not real in an Ultimate sense (and therefore not real at all, because the Ultimate is the Only Real).

Let's take the most obvious example from your direct experience right now. Look at the closest physical, visual object that you can see. Anything will do. These words, this page, or anything else in your peripheral vision while you keep reading (or read the instructions, stop, and then do the exercise). According to hard-fact science, by the time light reflects off of this object, enters your visual cortex, gets interpreted through your brain and conditioning and registers as "this thing," you're already seeing the past. That's right, *you're looking into the past*. It feels instantaneous because it's so fast, and we take it for granted because it's how we're taught, but think about it—the entire process of perception takes time, therefore by the "time" it's finished, you're not seeing the same object!

Here's an easier example, that we all remember from school days: A lightyear is the distance that light travels (at the speed of light, obviously) in one year.[58] If a star in our sky is six billion light-years away, technically (and very literally) speaking, we are seeing what that star looked like six billion years ago, itself having already "moved on" another six billion years or died already, and therefore we are seeing only the light reflected back...a phantom of what was... an "illusion." The star literally, physically, is not there anymore.[59] So, when we perceive anything that has measurement, we are seeing a shadow of the object that *seems* to be here, now. What we are in fact perceiving is an image projected out and reflected back from consciousness and displaying on the screen of our mind (through the visual cortex or whatever other sensory organs we are using. As we already mentioned, relative here and now is different from Ultimate Here and Now.[60] This place is see-through. And who are you who sees through?

Another reason it is very important to know the difference between relative and Ultimate is because *if it has a beginning and end in time and space (and is therefore relative), then* **you are not that**. What we identify with (and as) is who or what we say we are, namely, the one called "I." This may sound "duh-redundant," but slow it down and think about it. Often, we are swept away in a certain emotion or story or commentary or worry or even ex-citement or feel-good or excitement,[61] and the ego (more on the ego in the ego section) convinces us that we *are* that thing, or if not *we are that thing*, it convinces us that that thing is something to make real, or treat as Ultimately something that defines you or something that has more weight than it actually does on your life. More on all of this in the Who Am I? section, but for now, if it is relative, you are not it, by definition, because you are aware of it (if you can be aware of something, the something is not you); you are that which is aware of the the entire relative realm in the first place. See what I'm saying? Try it out. Anything you can observe, see, feel, experience, witness, touch, and for all intents and purposes *measure,*[62] is (and I will say it *ad nauseum*) relative, and therefore *not you*; because *you are that which is doing the observing, seeing, feeling, witnessing, touching, and measuring.*

Pack Your 'Chute Before You Jump

Before we get to some of the specific different flavors of Ultimate, I would like to make a few more pointers, just to be sure the cognitive pump has been primed up to par—sort of the final words of advice before you fall out of the plane.

Though there most certainly is a correlate in the body, and in the brain, when you are "in" one of the Ultimates, the Ultimates technically are not states of consciousness in the strict sense. We could call them perhaps Ultimate States, as long as you don't confuse that with relative states (including waking, dreaming, and deep sleep, and their meditative counterparts), which come and go like all states and all relatives, and which, to induce intentionally require implementing a technique, and still require a trigger of some sort to arrive there (and then the shift in body and brain wave occurs). When the state is "over," the body and the brain changes, and you are no longer there, even if the effects are lingering in your system and memory.

The Ultimate States, however, *never go anywhere*—"you" do,[63] in your relative, finite identity, attention, and center of gravity. In the same way that the sun does not turn off at night, but from your relative geographical perspective it seems to because the Earth has turned its back on the sun (this is of course very figurative, but is a great example and analogy), you, if you are identified with your relative, finite, personality self can turn your back on your Ultimate I Am Presence Self; but that Ultimate Self never goes anywhere, and is always "still there" when "you" turn around and face it; then, with enough practice, you become That, and a new You is born.

So, though there may be a correlation in the body and the brain of the finite self when it is in touch with the Ultimates *consciously,*[64] and though paradoxically a slight and subtle movement is required to "turn and look," (that is, until you never turn away again, but when you are first starting out, a little, or a lot, of effort is necessary) when you do turn and look, it is universally confirmed, if it is indeed the Ultimate, that "It" is always already the case. *If it is not, it is not!* It's that easy. And "you" cannot make it increase, cannot make it decrease, cannot make it be, cannot make it not be, cannot change it, cannot interrupt it. Again, however, you can interrupt your experience of it, your identity with it, the same as you can increase your experience of it, your identity with it, to the degree with which you evolve and grow as a finite self (more on this in the Who Am I? chapter).

Practice

Keeping all of the previous concepts and pointers from this chapter in mind, I have provided a list of koans that I have found helpful to trigger the Ultimates. Briefly, a koan is a phrase or a question, sometimes like a riddle, sometimes like an injunction or an instruction, that points to an Ultimate reality (or in my terms, a particular flavor of *the* Ultimate Reality). They comprise a genre of pointings that inherently point beyond themselves. They are not to be answered on the level of the question if it's a question (if to be answered at all), and not even to be enjoyed linguistically, artistically, or poetically. They are also not mantras or affirmations; that's a-whole-nother ballgame altogether. If received and responded to appropriately, the only answer is to simply be in the state induced by the koan.

It helps, however, to have a cognitive understanding, at least in theory, of what is being pointed to (hence, the information in this chapter), and to have at least a desire, if not an already established experience, for the general direction in which to aim. Once, at our

Sunday Gathering, I had given a shorter version of this list to the students as a homework assignment between our meetings. I asked them to take one each day and return to it throughout the day, ruminate on it, contemplate it, and come back next time we were together with their experiences, thoughts, questions, and insights. I was expecting a roomful of enlightened yogis and wide-eyed transformed consciousnesses; but when we reconvened a couple of weeks later, they had indeed done the homework, but they were incredibly frustrated. "These don't make any sense!" "I can't figure them out!" "What do these even mean?!" "That was very frustrating!" So, I spent twenty or so minutes dropping them into the Ultimate flavor of Pure Awareness with improvised guidance, and then I said, "Okay, stay in this interior space, get out your koan list, and we're going to read them again one at a time together." As we did, "Oohhh!" and "Wow! Now I get it!" were exclamations heard 'round the room. Then a profound stillness washed over the group as they dropped in one by one to the vibratory frequency provided by each koan. To this day, it was probably one of the most memorable experiences of the Ultimate (if not their first ever) that most of them had (or have) ever had. And it was certainly a learning experience for me as a teacher.

So, these require a cognitive as well as experiential understanding of what's being pointed to, or at least an acknowledgment of the intention and purpose of this kind of genre and how to work with it. As I said, and as I invited my students, I recommend that, at least to start, you take one per day, let it be in the back of your mind, sometimes bringing it to the forefront for conscious contemplation, and apply it to as many situations throughout the day as you can, not overtly omitting anything. You may also choose to stick with the same one for more than one day, if it is particularly potent and doing its work on you. I would not recommend more than one per day (until they are all solidly established), and I certainly do not recommend merely reading through them mindlessly like a social media feed (or again, even like a poem that stimulates the mind). It's also quite appropriate to set aside time for a seated meditation in which one koan (and its Ultimate flavor) is the focus of attention; but again, not as a mantra, and not to replace the meditation practice prescribed in the Meditation chapter. It's not even necessary to remember them word for word; simply remember the essence, or rewrite the words to suit your unique experience of it (but not because you're "not getting it"). Another way of saying it is *let the words read you*. Then, after a round of that, which will take at least a month, they will be nicely rooted in the soil of your subconscious, the pathway back to them on your own will be more clear cut, and you can do it again or be creative in how to utilize them on your own from then on.[65]

Note that some of the koans are pretty common and universal across traditions, and some are inspired by my practice and "made up" by me. Of the ones that are common and universal, I did not copy and paste them verbatim from any other source, and no one explicitly taught them to me. They're just the truth of the truth, and accessible in the invisible ethers for anyone who looks. Since the publication of this book, I am adding to the list as I receive more and refining the language to meet the responses and feedback of students; so stay tuned for that.

Be aware that the ego can confiscate, well anything, especially true, liberated seeing, so incorporate the other Basics along with this koan exercise, and be sure that it's really the Ultimate, and not just a really profound relative or a low-stage ego or a wounded subpersonality. To assist with this, along with the list of koans, I have provided a list of what each one looks like when hijacked in this way and a list of what the relative counterfeit of each looks like. Since there are more than a few different flavors, take your time (they aren't going anywhere!)— for beginner's level, simply access the Ultimate Itself (as opposed to relative) in whatever way, and get acclimated to that; for more advanced, feel into the differences, the textures, the uniqueness of the many Samadhis. Again, to the one just starting out, some of these may sound like the same thing, and that's okay. But upon further investigation, there are subtle and profound distinctions, which is why, of course, different words are used to reference them in the first place!

First, a description of the relative vs Ultimate version of each (this table you can read through; this is not the one-per-day practice):

	Relative	Ultimate
General Description	*requires focus, effort *changes *comes and goes *accomplished by relative self *beginning/end in time/ space *varies in degrees of measure *achieved *have to take steps to arrive *contrived *have to evoke it *can increase/decrease *conditional, conditioned *can be or not be	*effortless *always already *unchanging *experienced *by* relative self *expressed *through* relative self *impersonal but specific to person *received *don't have to go anywhere to arrive *spontaneous *cannot make it be or not be *complete unto itself *unconditional, unconditioned *never not been
Witness	*observation mode of mind *can be witnessed *sees this *not* that *must strive to remain neutral	*not a mental mode; beyond mind *cannot be witnessed *sees all things at once *neutral as its essence
Nonduality	*balance of opposites *still a boundary line *connecting 2+ objects *two becoming united *seeks acceptance of all	*no opposites *no boundary between *no separation that needs connection *two become one remain two *exclusion not an option

Boundless(ness)	*reckless, careless *bound vs released *limitation vs permission *"free-spirited" *no boundaries respected	*no line between subject/object *no line outside of Subject *Freedom/Liberation as Itself *All Things as Themselves *No Boundary possible
Present Moment	*this moment *in time* *must focus to "stay present" *don't worry about the future *don't analyze the past *no plans, no regrets	*This Moment beyond time *Now is all there is (no focus needed) *future is projection from Now *past is memory from Now *plan possibilities, for-give belief in time
Silence	*quiet/imperceptible sound *"natural" environment *not talking/whispering *minimal noise pollution	*That Which sustains sound waves *not dependent on environment **See endnote*[66] *interior, not exterior
Stillness	*little to no movement *scenic sunset *effect of easeful breath *rigid, frozen bodymind	*The Unmoving behind all movement *Steady Unchanging Stream *Space between forms *That-Which-Is after all rise and fall

Aloneness	*isolation, seclusion *psycho-physical perspective *spatial/geographic reference *loneliness possible *with or without "others" *degrees of closeness/ proximity	*as Myself by Myself with Myself *beyond body-mind-persona *boundless as All-There-Is *communion with Self and All *never without an "other"/no "other *no distance
Oneness	*all of us together *"we're on the same page" *group cohesion *we understand each other *unity in diversity *everything is connected	*One without two, 1st without 2nd *Zero, no one *All That Is is all there is *not a cumulation of parts *fractalized holographic hall of mirrors *same One in each
I Am-ness	*individuality *self-defined boundary *strong sense of person *uniqueness, "be yourself!"	*deepest sense of self *no boundary outside of Me *everyone's name is "I" *I Am the Center (non-locational)
Awareness	*attention vs distraction *focus vs lazy *clarity vs cloudy *learn new information *more pieces included *out of sight out of mind	*That Which registers phenomenal *cerebral component of 1st person *the Scanner that creates reality *out of mind out of manifestation *co-creative capacity *looking/receiving, active/passive

Presence	*as opposed to absence *here rather than there *to "be there for someone" *"stay present!" *to stay rather than leave *missing vs lost vs found	*Present even when absent or, *absence not possible *still Here when there *See endnote[67] *embodied component of Witness/I *never-lost-never-found
Beingness	*to be this rather than that *quality of existence *to live and not die *emotional state *animated bandwidth	*cannot make yourself not Be *primordial existence, Existence Itself *Life in All Things, even death *holds all beings/ Ground of Being *Why is there some-thing not nothing?
Consciousness	*alertness *waking state *functional vs fainting vs coma *degree of self-reflexiveness	*1st person Divine Intelligence *Awakeness through all states *the "Stuff" the "stuff" is made of *Single thread through all things
Nothing(ness)	*nihilism, depressed, pessimism *devoid of something, lacking *zero as opposed to numbers *to "not have"	*no object, no subject, but I *Void, Causal realm *no thing particular, all things Ultimate *Where did the some-thing come from?

Empty(ness)	*fulfilled vs unfulfilled
	*emaciated vs full
	*emotionally bereft
	*energy vs depletion
	*strength/vitality vs
	  weakness
		*filled by well that does
		  not run dry[68]
		*no-thing can fill it,
		  filled by All Things
		*Open Mind with no
		  preconception
		*"Not my will but
		  Thine be done"
		*limp dishrag[69]

Meaningless(ness)	*postmodern
	  deconstruction
	*Kafka, Camus, et. al.[70]
	*despair vs purpose
	*"you mean everything
	  to me"
		*Meaning beyond
		  human definition
		*See endnote[71]
		*See endnote[72]
		*See endnote[73]

And now the koans (and their ego counterfeit):

Koan	Ego
I am the only one (who has ever been) aware of anything	I am all that matters
Everything that has ever arisen has arisen in my awareness	Only my limited perception is real
Nothing has ever arisen outside of my awareness	I refuse to take the perspective of other people into account
Within without without	Huh?
I cannot be certain that other autonomous subjects exist	I look out for number one
All other so-called subjects exist as objects in my awareness	Objectification and abuse of "the other" (animals, the planet, racism, sexism, etc.)
I am aware of the body, therefore I am not the body	I don't have to take care of the body
I am aware of the mind, therefore I am not the mind	I am not responsible for my thoughts
I am aware of the personality (and subpersonalities), therefore I am not the personality (or subpersonalities)	I can act however I want
I am aware of the ego, therefore I am not the ego	I don't have to do shadow work
I cannot draw a line between where I end and "others" begin	Inappropriate (or no) boundaries; "Video Game Syndrome" (i.e., nothing is real); carelessness
I cannot draw a line between where I end and body/mind/personality/subpersonalities/ego begin, therefore I am not-other than (or separate from) the body/mind/personality/subpersonalities/ego	I'm not concerned about how my projections affect others

I am Alone	Nobody understands me. I isolate myself in shallow, spiritual bliss. I am more enlightened than anyone. *Or*, I'll never get it. I'll never be healed. No one loves me.
I am never alone	I am always bombarded. I can't escape.
If a tree falls in the forest, and I am not around to see it, does it fall?	out of sight out of mind; ignorant avoidance
If I am not around to see it, Is there even a tree? A forest? An I?	First-World naivete; there are no starving kids, no rape victims, nothing outside of my bubble
I have always been Here; past and future happen Now	I am excused for past mistakes and can perpetuate bad habits. Eat, drink, be merry, spend money, sleep around. No need to make a change in my life, for tomorrow is not guaranteed
How did I arrive Here?	Well, I drove!
If I trace my steps through memory, there are only fragments and frames	The story of my life doesn't matter. *Or* I have convenient amnesia because I live in the "present moment."
Silence behind every sound	I am only happy in environments that are quiet. *Or* Silence is awkward.
Stillness beneath every movement	Translated into rigidity, not moving. *Or* I am only happy when I'm sitting. *Or* I am only happy when I'm moving.
I cannot make myself not Be; I cannot turn Awareness off	It just "is what it is"; resignation
I cannot draw a line the other side of which I am not	I am the most important being on the planet and in all of the cosmos.

I Am the Center of the Universe	I am the center of the universe
I am in communion with all sentient beings	I want to have sex with everything and everyone.
All beings are sentient and conscious (including...)	Not rocks!
Nothing means anything	I can make up my own rules.
Every thing is Empty	I have no purpose.
I have never done anything	I don't have to do anything.
I have never gone anywhere	I don't have to go anywhere.
Nothing can be added to or taken from this moment	There is no such thing as free will.
I cannot do anything outside of God's will	I feel trapped
Stop trying!	I don't wanna!

Taking Responsibility

———◆———

Just as in all the other chapters and sections of this book, one of my primary intentions is to define and differentiate various terms and phrases that are either otherwise not understood by the average person, are used interchangeably with another word or phrase when in actuality there is something important to note by knowing the specific meaning of each word that most folks think "mean the same thing," or are so commonly used even in our pop-culture language (not to mention our religious/spiritual language) that we've lost the essence of what the first person who used the word was trying to say...this chapter is no different, and is possibly the most important in this regard due to the many (mis)understandings and (mis)uses and (ir)regularity of words like personality, ego, shadow, and false self, and projection, just to name a few. What do these words mean anyway? Are they in fact the same thing? Is it mere semantics? Can they be mashed into a single category that translates simplistically to "the bad part of ourself"? Are they even bad? Is there such thing as evil? Is the ego evil? Is the ego the devil inside? What about our personality? What's that? Or relative, finite, conventional self? These questions and more will be answered—at the very least implied and approached—in this chapter.

It's important for writers and teachers of this kind of work to define their terms (which is just what I'm doing) so that their students and readers may not make grand assumptions based on their own preconceived ideas and preloaded reference points from other sources and miss the entire point of what's being said. It's important that we teachers and writers ourselves know precisely what we are trying to say and what we are meaning when we choose to use the word *ego* instead of *shadow* or instead of *false self*, etc., rather than lumping them into an unsophisticated heap. Otherwise we are doing a disservice (or at least conveying only a shallow, one-dimensional, presumptive, cliche picture) to the masses we are hoping to reach.

Ego

Let's start with the ever-elusive ego, probably the most demonized and misunderstood of the bunch. As with any word, it needs to be contextualized, and could of course mean many things, depending on who's using it and what's being said. A Course In Miracles, for example, has a particular way that it uses the word, and a unique-to-itself meaning behind it, and stays with that meaning throughout. Eckhart Tolle, one of the first that I, back in the day, heard use the word ego consistently to point to a specific phenomenon, has a slightly different approach. Ken Wilber uses the term egocentric. What are these all trying to say? For scholars and serious students, it's important. Again, just as we said in the Ultimates chapter, for the novice, it's more excusable to simply understand the category and not need to split hairs and parse out the subtleties; but for the more advanced practitioner, it's vital.

So, as with our What is meditation? question, when asking ten people on the street what the ego is, you'd potentially get ten different answers (or a few categorically expected ones; but more than one nonetheless). What would you say it is? Stop and think about it for a moment. Even if you've already read this book once, even if you've heard me or others say it a hundred times, don't just mentally blurt out an answer—for your understanding of the ego is likely to have changed since the last time you thought about it (if you've ever thought about it). My perspective certainly has changed over the years, and has done so mostly because of my own direct engagement with the ego rather than aloof, ethereal theories alone—it's called evolution of consciousness and maturity of experience y'all. If you blindly follow a teacher or dogma or system or school of thought, the definitions may stay the same over time and may not even fit your actual perception; but if you do the work yourself, it'll change over time due to your first-hand relationship with the thing in question. So, what's the ego to me?

The word ego (in Latin) and ἐγώ (in Greek) simply means "I."[74] This realization is harmless enough on the surface, but upon further investigation has great implications for our study here. Which I is speaking, for example, and about whom is it speaking in the sentence, "I can't believe what I just did to myself!" How many I's are there? The I's are hiding in plain sight! I, in fact, is one of the most commonly used words, in all human languages, but it's rare that the speaker, who is speaking as I, is aware of which I they are coming from. I is everyone's name for themselves too.

All of this is common knowledge; but have you ever thought about it? When you say I, is it the personality or finite I? Is it the ego I? Is it the Great I Am I? How about this sentence for example: *I remember when I was a kid, I was afraid that one day I would end up all by myself with no one to talk to.* Or this one: *I want to be a part of something bigger than myself.* Can you identify the various uses of I? Is it the same one? Look closely, and don't take it for granted. Who is speaking? Who is being spoken about? And who is aware of the one speaking about the one who is being spoken about?

Who is the one presently remembering the one in the past who had thoughts about one in the future?...or Who is aware of the one already bigger than the one that wants to be a part of something bigger than itself?...

The grammar gives it away! Remember in school when you learned about the subject, object, direct object, and indirect object of a sentence? Or 1st-person pronouns and reflexive pronouns? You never thought such information would be useful for the spiritual journey did you? Needless to say, and back to our point, as long as the teacher, writer, scholar, student, *or common person*, knows what they mean when they use certain words, we have no problem! But can you see how there are so many possibilities of miscommunication, and why it matters, around a word as seemingly insignificant (but probably the most powerful word in any language) as I? Who's talking? To whom is that one talking? Who is that one talking about? And who is aware of all of this?

In any case, Freud meant one thing by ego, or *Ich*, Eckhart Tolle means one thing by ego, Ken Wilber means one thing by ego, *A Course In Miracles* means one thing by ego (and because I have studied each, I can tell you they are all in the same ballpark and at the same time distinctly different). So what do I mean by ego? My understanding (and use) of the word, and thus my experience of ego, comes from an amalgam of all of the above plus my own engagement, contemplation, and work with it in my life and practice.

Here it is: For me, the ego is not its own I as such, but is the very principle of separation that will utilize any already-established I (including personality, subpersonality, relative self or Ultimate Self) or nexus-knot as a platform to pitch its agenda.

A full comprehension, at least intellectually, and hopefully experientially, of this must be preceded by the knowledge, insight, and understanding that *Ultimately there is no separation, anywhere, ever*— which means an experience of the Ultimates, in particular in this case Awareness, Nonduality, and Boundlessness is absolutely vital (see the table in the Ultimates chapter), and which means you know from the start the ego is lying and playing games.[75] If you have <u>not</u> seen, *from the Ultimate perspective*, that separateness (and along with separateness, lack, deficiency, boundaries, need, etc.) literally does not exist, then you are probably already operating, possibly without knowing it, from an egoic state or perspective, however "spiritual" or mature or evolved you may be or think you are.

Let's try it real quick. I'd like for you to see it, at least a glimpse, before we continue. Notice a few things in your awareness right now (could be physical, mental, emotional, energetic, interior, or exterior; any *thing*). From the standpoint of Ultimate Awareness, can you draw a line where awareness ends and these things begin? Wait for it...wait for it...No! Every *thing* arises *in* and *as* Your Awareness (not as the bodymind, but Awareness Itself). Therefore, no separation. Anywhere. Ever. Now, get a sense for your sense of *self* right now. Who you call "I." The one sitting right there reading this. From the standpoint of Ultimate Awareness, can you draw a line where awareness ends and this "I" begins? Survey says...NO! Next, from the perspective of Ultimate Awareness, is the perception of this I arising in the same seamless space as the other "things"? If you said Yes, you'd be right! Ding-Ding-Ding! Okay—Expand and extrapolate those injunctions and that understanding out everywhere, in all directions, all dimensions and beyond, inside and out, and see if you can find a place where Awareness is not. Awareness simply follows (or the things follow Awareness, or Awareness and the things go spontaneously simultaneously hand-in-hand)! There is nowhere it is not, there is nowhere YOU are not, as That, and no boundary between That, You, and Any-Thing (capital letters or not)!

Now, of course, I need to say this: *Relatively*, boundaries are of the utmost importance. And (and this is a tricky one) the ego can confiscate an Ultimate realization such as the Nondual Boundless Awareness that you just glimpsed (or are still soaking in) and actually implant its function of separateness by lying to you and saying you don't need healthy boundaries as a relative self.

But back to what I was saying. Another way by way of analogy or illustration of this Nondual Boundless Awareness, just to be sure you get it, at least conceptually, is this: Think of a quilt. Like Grandma's cozy quilts that have multiple textures, colors, fabrics, pictures, and seams and threads and borders *within it*. There may even be three-dimensional shapes that lift out of the two-dimensional flatness to give it character. My grandma made the most beautiful quilts, with a detail and intricacy, and love and care, such that it would take months to go over completely and still not discover all the little messages and memories and inside jokes encoded that only the person it's made for would fully understand. Do you have something in mind like that? Remember, this is an analogy. It will only go so far, but it works quilt (I mean quite) well. What if that quilt, and all the content and details and texture and fabric and little meanings and messages and beauty and perfection and quirkiness was "made with love from Grandma" just for YOU! Intimately for you. And because it's specially sewn for you, and the meaning is known by only you, it's a *part* of you, and the sentimental value is priceless because it can't be cherished in the same way by anyone *but* you. Here are some questions: *From the perspective of the quilt, is there any separation between it and all the things it's made of,* or *can you draw a line where quilt ends and details of the quilt begin? Or From the perspective of the meaning stitched into the fabric, can you draw a line where you end and it begins?* Again, No! I hope you're getting this now. The seams themselves (which relatively seem to make boundaries between this thing and this thing and to hold all the pieces together) are themselves a seamless part of the whole quilt. And the love and meaning from Grandma through the quilt to you cannot be parsed out either—are not separate.

So it is with *everything in existence, including your personal sense of I as well as the transpersonal I (and even including God, represented by Grandma).* I see it as one vast seamless, boundaryless, extending-in-all-directions-and-times-and-spaces-and-places-and-dimensions tapestry. You are not separate from "All That Is"; you are both part of All That Is and aware of All That Is, and All That Is is always already perfect, whole, and complete. In other words, there is nothing that is not the tapestry; nothing outside the tapestry.

And guess what. The ego is also a perfect piece of the tapestry; a seamless seam, a stitched-in pattern, woven for a purpose, which we'll see in a moment. But what makes the ego unique is that it itself is not a fixed square so to speak of the quilt; it can move around to whatever section of the tapestry it wants and attempt to put a choke hold on it, tempting you to believe that what it's choking off and emphasizing is separate from the rest. It's a lie from the start. As we just saw, the ego itself is not even separate from the All-That-Is tapestry, but it has cunning ways to deceive you into thinking *it* is, and *you* are, and whatever *thing* it chooses to focus its attention on is too. It always has a strong opinion about itself, or you, or that thing. It tries to convince you, and everyone and everything else in the tapestry, that it is special, needs something, lacks something, might lose something, wants something to be different, and is ultimately separate.[76]

Stories & Lies

To boil it down even more, the ego tells stories as its primary spell-casting tactic to whisper in your ear. Its stories are either about attachment or aversion, allergy or attraction, like or dislike, adding or subtracting, need or desire. If it can convince you that you like a particular thing so much that you manipulate the tapestry and push everything else away to get it, or to keep it...or that you want to avoid a particular situation at all costs...or to fixate on one thing and forget all other things...or that something could possibly go wrong or be against you...or that there is such thing as an outside force that could harm you or be against you.[77] When these stories land and are reinforced, the ego has you in its snare of separateness and fear, which inevitably causes pathological suffering.

So, to use the quilt analogy again, it would be like taking a piece of string and tying it around a balled-up chunk of the fabric or putting a frame around just one of the squares or painting one of the squares black in order to either on the one hand enjoy it at the expense of all the others, keep it all to yourself, or on the other hand try to get rid of it, cut it out, or ignore it. Does it work? Not only does it not work, but it's a waste and a drain of vital energy and actually creates the opposite effect—makes the whole thing worse. Not to mention, Grandma put it there just for you![78] In squeezing the life out of one of the parts of the quilt as the most important, or trying to keep it crystallized as it is,[79] your perception of that part is cramped, because, well, there's a rope tied around it! Why not enjoy its beauty as intended, and not with a choke hold. Or in trying to get rid of a particular, unwanted piece, if you did succeed, by crumpling it up, or even tearing it out, it would cease being the quilt it was created to be (a contradiction/paradox: even the cuts now become a part of the fabric)! So in the same way as we asked the question, *Can you draw a line where the quilt ends and the fabric begins?*, we could ask now, *Can you cut out a piece of the quilt and keep the quilt the quilt?*

And the stories you tell yourself, fed by the ego, cause you not to be able to see reality any other way. Take a moment and translate the quilt analogy into your life, and into what it means for Ultimate Reality, if you haven't already, and allow the implications to sink in...

What the Devil?

Now, the question always comes, is the ego bad? Are we trying to get rid of the ego? Is the ego our enemy? Is it a *keep your friends close and your enemies closer* sort of thing? Can you learn from the ego? Is the ego the devil?

Well, in the New Testament, the "devil" in Greek is διάβολος, (or in Spanish, diablo, or where we get our word diabolical). Guess what διάβολος means etymologically. Something like "the one who throws against." The first part of the word, δία (pronounced *dia*), has different meanings depending on the word it is coupled with; and in this case, it means "against." The second part of the word is a conjugation from βάλλω (pronounced *ball-o*), which, it doesn't take much imagination to see, is where we get our word "ball" from—hence, to throw! In the Kabbalah, the same meaning is applied to the one called "the Opponent." It's actually not evil, per se.[80] Seen from this perspective, the ego, then, is that principle that Whoever Made The Tapestry decided to weave into it in order to challenge us; and thus, provoke us to grow, evolve, and transform.

Unfortunately, if we do not have the right vision and approach and relationship to this principle, the consequences can be dire. There is an often-quoted, and in Magic/Mythic Christian circles often-misused, Bible passage, Malachi 2:16: "'...I hate divorce,' says the LORD...'" From a higher level of interpretation, this is not talking about signing divorce papers at a local courthouse. Very interestingly (and coincidental to our quilt analogy), the next part of the verse says, "...and covering one's garment with violence." The garment! And violence with the garment would be the ego's choke-holds. On a deeper-than-literal level, what it's saying is that from the perspective of "God," or "the Ultimate," there is no such thing as divorce, aka *separation*; the Mind of God cannot even conceive of it. And it is violent to believe, or attempt, otherwise. And yet, if we believe the lies of the ego, that there could possibly be separation, or divorce, then "actual" violence (and war and rape and hunger and desolation and murder) will be all over our quilt. And that's how the innocent sparring partner becomes an enemy—and it need not be that way.

However, if we have the right vision of this opponent, as well as an Ultimate realization of Nondual Oneness (seeing through the eyes of God the inconceivability of separation or lack or deficiency or need), it is easily dismantled. So it's not something we are trying to get rid of, but rather to recognize, put into proper perspective, and diminish its operative function, thus passing its jests and tests. It's a seamless part of the tapestry, and is either friend or foe based on your relationship with it, but just know that its existence does indeep depend on a fundamental lie. For me, out of the vast, spacious Oneness That Always Already Is, its voice manifests as a temptation to believe a part of it is not That; saying, "What about this?" "Or that thing?" "Do you want to make this part more important?" "Will you shun this piece?" "How about be afraid of something?" "Believe that something could possibly go wrong? Harm you?" And I simply have to remember how to release the contraction, not buy the lie, and return to the Vastness that I am and that has never not been.

The ego, as it infiltrates a host site (because, remember, it will use anything), barricades itself in and walls everything else out (paradoxically though, the walls too are...you got it...a seamless part of the whole perfection), will then create an entire narrative to feed you and everyone else to convince you to keep it living, breathing, and breeding. You will now be keen to it, however, because all of its "suggestions" come from some variety of lack-need, attack-defense, or separation in general. Lack. Need. Attack. Defense. Separation. That's the ego's m.o. Learn to detect it. And if it can be seen as kind of an interior muscle spasm, your interior muscle development eventually becomes far stronger than that (and more on this in the Interior Domain chapter), and the spasm softens and releases.

So the verdict is still out on whether the ego ever goes away permanently. Ask me on my deathbed. What I can say is it can be permanently dislodged as a primary source of suffering, it can be permanently disidentified from, and it can definitely be diminished in its frequency and intensity. If you implement the Five Basics on a daily (and moment-to-moment) basis, it'll happen. I promise. And this, in particular, is taking great responsibility for your own healing, and thus removing one more ego from the world's great suffering.

Projection & Reflection

You've probably heard the word projection before. You probably, just like all the other terms in this book, have a current understanding of what you suppose it means in mind. You've probably even used the word defensively with a partner, friend, or loved-one: "Don't project your shit onto me!" The standard definition comes from the world of psychoanalysis, and may not be far from what you'd say it is. In essence, projection is the phenomenon indicating that that which bothers you most about another is actually something that bothers you about yourself but that you've become unaware of in yourself; and conversely, that which you admire or worship most in another is actually a quality about yourself that you already have but have lost touch with. Simple enough. But the question that concerns us here is *why*. The why deeply intertwines with all of the other Basics, and I will now show how.

First and foremost, from the perspective of Ultimate I Am-ness, or Awareness, or Oneness, pointed to by the koan *I am the only one (who has ever been) aware of anything*, straightaway it is seen that there is Ultimately no such thing as an "other."[81] All so-perceived "others" are not only a seamless part of the Tapestry of Your Awareness, but are uniquely customized projections of your own subconscious.[82] Because I believe (and not only I, but all authentic interior traditions) that this place, however conceived, is Benevolent, loving, and *for you*,[83] I believe (not only from theory but also my own experience) that everything is set up specifically for each individual's healing and liberation. This means the Universe, or God, or the Heavenly Father Hologram, or Higher Wisdom/Intelligence, or what-have-you-whatever-you-call-It wants you to resolve all past wounds (aka samskara aka nexus-knots) and have *Ultimate* abiding peace and freedom and Union with Itself (aka enlightenment aka samadhi). But in order for this to happen, you have to feel (remember *peel—>reveal—>feel—>heal?*) everything that has otherwise been ignored, suppressed, demonized, and avoided. But for some deeply primordial, or merely conditioned, reason, we are afraid (and sometimes completely unable or unwilling) to "come clean" with a sober, honest acknowledgement about what's really going on inside. So, because (at least) the third-dimensional Earth plane operates like a fractalized hall of mirrors, what is most relevant for you to come in contact with in yourself is what you will primarily see outside of yourself...until you "own" it, take responsibility for it, bring back what you previously "gave away," and reintegrate the fragments into the whole. As projection goes both ways, it could be, again, something painful or something beautiful—but it will continue to be "out there," probably causing some kind of discomfort or suffering, until you take responsibility for it "in here."

Basically your reflection is all you see everywhere you look, colored by the lens of whatever unresolved trauma or drama still resides in your sub/unconscious, held into place by stories that you tell yourself or lies you have bought about the Ultimate Reality. Ever feel like the same pattern repeats over and over again in your life? This is likely why. It's a feedback loop. And this is different from the way a lot of New Age spiritual teachers teach the same information. Often it is depicted as "your fault" for not doing something right—you're having doubting thoughts or lack mentality, so you should tape a mantra or affirmation on your computer screen or your bathroom mirror and repeat over and over to yourself how much you love yourself and how much you believe in abundance and wealth. It doesn't work. Ask anyone who's tried. And if it does, it only works on the surface level like a magnetic magic trick, but the ego, and thus the suffering, stays lodged deep down and can live to die another day. What I say is that the Good Heavenly Father Hologram *wants* you to succeed, *wants* you to see yourself and your projections reflected back, so it allows you to relate with them at arm's length at first...when you believe the emotion or the problem or the inspiration exists "outside" yourself. Sometimes, if the Hologram[84] is ready for you to get the lesson, it will turn up the heat and the feedback loop will repeat in shorter intervals and greater intensity.

But here's the fork in the road, the invitation, that's ultimately up to you to choose: If you are not privy to this knowledge, and how it relates to all Five Basics, you will probably become bitter, angry, and pessimistic about "the way things are," your "poor me" lot in life, and the "unfortunate" cards you've been dealt. If you do have an inkling that a communication is taking place, pointing you to true healing and liberation, all you have to do is say Yes (and continue putting in the work outlined in this book...and of surrender, commitment, and patience), and the rest is history. You are now on another timeline, you are now under the careful watch of a Divine Intelligence heretofore buried deep and dormant, now activated and tuned to the dial of your highest good, and the process of transformation you came here for has been catalyzed. What comes next is not up to you, and for once you do not want it to be, but could be the dawn of the dark night in which your very soul is readied for Union with God.[85]

Shadow

A quick word on another frequently used term that is, again, like the ego, usually interpreted as "the bad part." Hopefully you're beginning to see that, from a certain perspective, there are no bad parts; but there are parts that need work and that indeed cause tremendous (and unnecessary) suffering that potentially lead to "bad" things in the world and in your life. This tendency for a molehill to become a mountain, so to speak, is particularly evident when we talk about why the shadow is called the shadow and just how it operates. Think of the shadows made by trees, or clouds, or mountains for that matter when the sun is low in the sky. Or the shadow your own body makes on a full-moonlit night with a clear sky. The reason there's a shadow in the first place is what?—*because there's a light source, and an object that blocks the light from getting to a place it wants to shine on.* I may not even need to go further into explaining the correlation with the psycho-spiritual shadow. But I'll give a bit more. The shadow is always bigger than the actual object, isn't it? And sometimes the object, and the ground, is *overshadowed.* And sometimes you can be afraid of your *own* shadow! Drawing the parallels now?

There's a Sanskrit word, *Purusha,* from the Vedas and Upanishads, which refers to your deepest I-Am Consciousness which *gives light* to everything arising in your awareness. Think about it. Behind your physical eyes, beyond your brain, beneath your soul, there must be *Something, Someone,* none other than your very Self in the 1st-Person which literally lights up the world! In the beginning, God said, "Let there be light," and there was light! And after there was Light, God made the world for the Light of Awareness to see. The ancient Yogic and Hindu texts also have incredibly complex and detailed descriptions of the process that ensues from there. There is a *mind field* they call the *citta* (pronounced *chitta*) which is where the images of the "exterior" objects are displayed—it's a movie screen! Or even better, it's the film that the interference pattern is projected onto in a hologram. It's phenomenologically scientific; directly perceived and confirmed. We've just now begun to understand how right they were; but for some reason, we needed it to be "proven" and extrapolated into third-person lab experiments on rats' neural pathways.

As we've seen, You Are the Only One Aware of Anything, therefore the Inner Light is You! But as we've also seen, lots of rips and tears and trauma and drama and contraction happen to the things in front of your Awareness. You become identified with the changeful world of form, you think you are something you are not, you try to hold on to something you can't, and life throws curveballs. It's nobody's fault; it's the way of the game for now. But nonetheless, by whatever word, *samskaras* develop, and the ego contraction infiltrates the host site, and subpersonality monsters are born. Because these are not *natural*, but are imposed and added in an artificial, non-organic way, in my opinion (and there's the zinger), they cast shadow until fully processed and reintegrated into the whole system. And just like a physical shadow from objects blocking the sun, they block (or obscure) the Light of Awareness, and cause the original relatively manageable nexus-knot to become a full-blown problem that has to be wrestled with and worked out (and which causes more trouble than really necessary, for yourself and "others.") Also, it's often the shadow rather than the object itself that you relate (and struggle) with; not to mention that the object is an illusion already! So the shadow is doubly removed from the Truth.

To conclude this chapter, the holographic hall of mirrors is set up perfectly for your journey, and will respond in a way that seems benevolent or malevolent to the degree with which you learn to relate with it as such. It's Intelligent, Loving, and *for your healing and liberation* if you'll let it be and learn to see in a new way. The world's depravity begins and ends with you, and the promised Golden Age, or New Earth, is ushered in as one individual at a time takes responsibility like never before for themselves, and thus, returning projection to its proper source, releasing ego contraction back to the Vastness, and fully processing the snags and wounds which invariably hide in shadow that can only exist because there is Great Light on the other side.

Who Am I?
(& who am I not?)

---◆---

Ramana Maharshi is known to have said that the inquiry *Who am I?* is the only tool you need for your knapsack to attain enlightenment. That, along with what we might call the *identity epidemic*[86] that is rampant in our mainstream, and our spiritual, pop-culture these days, is why I have decided to give it its very own space as one of the Five Basics (and therefore dedicate an entire chapter to its meaning and implication). From my perspective, all Five are equally important, mutually inclusive, and none are more primary than the others.[87] As you're seeing, they all interrelate philosophically as well as pragmatically. Therefore, you could argue that Who Am I? could be dissolved into one or more of the others and thus have only four Basics; but that just ain't how I'm doin' it, and the first two sentences of this paragraph give my explanation for an entire chapter dedicated to this one.

Persona

It may go without saying, but I do not want to make any assumptions, and as I've said many times, the purpose of this book is to clarify some otherwise overlooked or overused terminology or taken for granted concepts, so, I want to make clear, that the consideration of *Who am I?* is dealing with *identity*, or *sense of self*. I've had some students, when introduced to this question, say things like, "Wow, I've never even thought about *who* I am!," or, "...what it *feels like* to be a self," or, "...what *kind* of self we're talking about," or, "...how many selves there are," or, "...that a self means more than a body," or, "...my identity is beyond the personality!"

You may think you know these things. But do you? Don't you often act as though you *are* your body-mind-persona self? As a quick example, when talking "about" yourself, don't you point to your body sometimes, or touch your chest? "Me!" But who? Who's you? Who's pointing? Or, "I brushed my teeth." Whose teeth? Who brushed? Or in yoga class even, we teachers like to say very misleading things like, "Move *your* hands away from yourself." What? Is that even possible? Who's moving what where here? Think about it... Of course the language would become quite cumbersome and awkward if the cue was, "Move the hands away from the torso." But from the perspective we're talking about here, it would be more accurate. Across the board, the way we perceive ourselves is built into the words we use on a daily basis.

Anyway. I have learned that many of the practices and inquiries and contemplations that I do very naturally, because it's "just what I do," do not come so naturally or easily to other people. So I'm happy to break it down slowly. Broadly speaking, when it comes to asking the basic question *Who am I?*, it is mostly important to recognize and remember the difference between, you guessed it, the Ultimate Self and the relative self (or selves).

Though I use the terms relative self, finite self, conventional self, and personality self more or less interchangeably, here I'd like to discuss specifically the origin of the word personality, or persona, and why it's helpful to contextualize just what the relative/finite/conventional self is (and is not) in general. Once again, I will ask you to pause a moment and answer the question, *What's a personality?* Don't glaze over it. You currently have an understanding and interpretation of what it means. What is that understanding and interpretation? If you said something like someone's unique characteristics, you'd be in the ballpark. But precisely because they are *unique*, which means *different* possibly from *person to person*, and *changing*, then you should automatically be triggered into knowing we're talking relative here, and by now you see why that's important to distinguish from the Ultimate. The words personality, persona, and person come from the Latin *personare* (pronounced *pair-so-nar-ay*, emphasis on the *nar*) and the Greek πρόσωπον (pronounced *pro-so-pone*, emphasis on the *pro*), both of which refer to a theatrical mask. Literally, this is the word, in Greek and Latin respectively, that was/is used to mean mask!

As a writer and lover of words myself, I like to say that *worlds make words, and words make worlds.* In other words... When a new experience happens (a world) and there is no word already in place to describe or indicate or reference or point to it, someone (or a group of someones) has to come up with one! And from then on, if it "sticks" as the standard placeholder for such experience or phenomenon or world (in whatever culture, even if it's only an inside word that has meaning for a married couple, or siblings, or as large as a nation or religion or through multiple generations), that word is ingrained into the collective psyche for ease of use later on. Problem is, it becomes so embedded into the *sub*conscious that we often use words without *really* knowing what they mean. Some very condescending phrases and words that have their roots in slavery or racism or masculine authoritarian abuse, for example, we have unconsciously inherited and mindlessly (by no fault of our own until we stop and look) use in everyday speech, which I won't repeat here. In any case, worlds (i.e., experiences, or phenomena, whether mundane or spiritual or practical or natural or what-have-you) make words (i.e, demand that, if they are to be shared later, must have a *signifier*, or physical sign/symbol, as it's called in linguistics), and thereafter and simultaneously, *words make worlds* (meaning, when that word is used again, and again-and-again, it calls forth the world, if "only" in the imagination[88] or the mind of the hearer to be shared with the sharer to know what's being said). Of course, one of the roles of the philosopher, the poet, the writer, the teacher is to shine new light on old concepts and paradigms and words, or styles and genres and modalities and approaches, especially the ones that have become worn out and unquestioningly repeated and passed down to the detriment and dilution of the intended purpose or meaning. *"Geez Kemper, can you just get on with the persona thing?"* Or did you even forget we were talking about the persona thing? Did you think I forgot? Welcome to my world of words. And welcome to my brain, which can sustain a long-winded thread of thought and never lose track or get off course. It's good for your brain's elasticity too. So stay with me, even if you have to slow it down and take one bite at a time!

So, okay. What I'm trying to say is that the first person who used the word *persona*, or *personality*, or *person* in English knew precisely what they were pointing to, and was making a direct reference to a mask. Three things are important here: (1) that you get to know what kind of mask you wear, (2) that you learn how to work with your particular mask and grow into the most mature version of it, and (3) that you never forget that you're wearing a mask in the first place, and always remember to ask *who's* wearing the mask!

There are many really good transformational systems that you can use to get to know your mask, or your character, if you will. The primary one that I have used over the years is the Enneagram. Other good ones are Human Design, and believe it or not, Ayurveda.[89] Whatever you choose, make sure it's a tool that will help you grow, become more mature, set you free from the shadow aspects of the mask, break you out of a fixed mold and not merely reinforce your identification with the mask. Most typical psychological "personality tests," or even New Age astrology that has become very popular these days, lock you into a particular "that's just who I am" box, give you permission to *not* take a closer look, and never challenge you to grow. If the system over-excitedly announces or promotes that you can now discover who you are!, in a pre-given always and ever sort of way, without a path laid out to change, be skeptical. "Oh, I'm a Capricorn, that's how we are, take it or leave it." Or, once I saw an advertisement for an Enneagram 6 support group—uhhh, that's like a gathering of alcoholics meeting up for cocktails to discuss addiction. If it's true and authentic, it will bring out all of your shadows, will more times than not be an uncomfortable, bumpy ride, and until they've been worked smooth, will pronounce the rough edges of your mask, and for a minute, the prescribed practices for your specific type will feel like the worst possible idea, and the "last thing in the world" you would want to do. But the point is, it's good medicine, and if you're honest with yourself, you know it, so you stick with it, and the reward makes the work worth it; every time.

The most intriguing aspect, to me, about the various systems, is that they do seem to operate from a kind of archetypal template, which not only indicates more evidence for some kind of holographic programmed reality (that we won't go into here), but also means that lots of groundwork has already been done over the centuries and millennia to lay out a path, a groove, for exactly how to grow.[90] In general, even if you don't utilize one of these systems, you can guarantee that such path, if it is genuine, and if it is initiated by the Intelligent Benevolence of the Heavenly Father Hologram (aka Universe aka God), it will align with the principle of *pratipaksha bhavana* referred to by Patanjali in the *Yoga Sutras*.[91] *Pratipaksha bhavana* is commonly translated as something like "cultivating the opposite."[92] One of the goals, in my opinion, of doing "work" on the relative self or persona, is to become the most mature version of that templated mask as possible; therefore, a sign of growth on that spectrum is less shadow and less pathology of your type. Each type has its own shadowy, immature, pathological manifestations, and therefore there are predictable and well-worn ways to grow out of those into maturity.[93] In a nutshell, what I'm saying is that *if the system or tool of transformation is a good one, it will prescribe for you to go against the grain of all of your pathological symptoms in order to get well.* The Enneagram does this, and again, believe it or not, Ayurveda does as well.

For example, I am a Nine on the Enneagram, the Peacemaker. A mature Peacemaker is a very easygoing, relaxed, go-with-the-flow kind of person; an immature Peacemaker is a lazy sloth that doesn't ever want to do anything and could just slob around all day. There was a time in my life in which I exhibited a pretty unhealthy, immature, pathological version of a Nine. Ironically, however, I've never been a slothful spiritual seeker or sojourner or practitioner. The slothfulness of my immature Nineness manifested solely as laziness around practical, physical, "third-dimensional" matters. Luckily, at that time, I was in the hands of an amazing and capable mentor who introduced me to the work of the Enneagram, and I began following its promptings to *cultivate the opposite* (before I even knew of Patanjali's parallel), which, for a Nine, is to consciously take on the positive characteristics of the self-motivated, go-getter mature Three. Again, and the reason why I went into the whole "no such things as opposites" thing in the endnote, on the Enneagram spectrum, the Three is not the "opposite" of a Nine, but it is the most vibratorily different, distinct, and dissonant enough that implementing its characteristics does indeed go against the grain of an immature Nine and expose the rough edges of slobbery pretty quickly.

Characteristics of a mature Three include: success-driven, ability to accomplish and achieve goals, task-mastery, and motivated to climb the ladder. In and of themselves, these are of course good qualities, but have immature versions as well for an actual Three person (same as easygoing walks a fine line with laziness). While we're at it, our collective American personality is a very immature and pathological Three— i.e., only practical matters matter, get ahead or fall behind, succeed at all costs, gain the whole world and lose your soul. Nonetheless, an immature, lazy, slothful Nine gets a much needed kick-in-the-ass by cultivating the opposite and accomplishing something. In this particular system, each number has its own prescribed path to wellness. So the prescription for the immature Three, for example, is, well, the "opposite" (like the Nine)—take a chill pill, let go of your to-do list for a day, be okay with where you are without always looking for advancement, relax! There are seven other numbers of course; but it would take more space than I want to dedicate here to go through all of them.[94]

The same principle approach to healing is found in Ayurveda. Of the three doshas, or constitutions (or for our purposes, masks, which in this case are sort of whole-body costume masks!), whichever one you are mostly oriented to, the understanding is that you already have "enough" of that one quality or essence—that your cup is already pretty full of, say, Earth energy, or Fire energy, or Air energy—so, much more of it will send you overboard. So Pittas, or those with primarily Fire energy, will tip over into high strung, everywhere-and-nowhere anxiety if they eat spicy foods, drink a lot of alcohol, or have lifestyles that are too active. They're already active; no chance of ever not being full of fire. Therefore, the Pitta's path to balance is to douse the fire a bit with cooling foods, and perhaps living in a colder climate or a small town with a slower pace. You get the idea. Eventually, you don't have to think about it. Eventually, you become not only the mature version of your specific type, but a "well-rounded" person, as they say, operating from and as the best of all the types. Eventually, after putting in the effort, you're simply returned to the natural, healthy, organic *person* God designed *you* to be, and it becomes more and more effortless from there.

And not only that. While it's fun to "figure out" what type you are in the various systems, and depending on, well, your personality itself, you may love how succinct and easy it is to categorize and work with the archetypes in the template (or conversely you may have a personality that rebels against anything that feels like being "put in a box," even though that's not what this is...), and while you have and are a body+/-, have and are a mind+/-, have and are a soul+/-, etc., if you continue to engage the Ultimates (in particular the Who Am I? Ultimate), the most important inquiry into your identity quickly becomes: *Okay, I have and am all of this and more than all of this; all of this is a mask that I wear; I can see that now. But wait a second... If this is a mask, who is wearing the mask (or, all of these masks)?!* It becomes commonplace to ask yourself, *Who's speaking? The mask, or the one behind the mask?*[95]

To illustrate further, I like to use the analogy of an actor and their character or role—the word persona does after all come from the world of theater, so why not extrapolate the meaning. A "good actor," they say, "loses themself" in the role. Maybe so, while on set; but if the actor can't remember to "disidentify" from the character (i.e., take the mask off) when filming is done, you get something like Heath Ledger allegedly committing suicide, or "losing himself" in the darkness of the Joker character in a depressive overdose, forgetting "who he was." (Un)fortunately, it was one of the most brilliantly convincing performances in any movie, as he "stole the show" every time he was on camera. But it cost him his life (theoretically). Jim Carrey also gave one of his most genius performances, and lost himself in his role, as Andy Kaufman, but was able to pull himself out after the final scene was shot.[96] Speaking of Jim Carrey, he once lost himself in the mask of a character who lost himself in a mask and eventually broke the spell of the mask and remembered his true identity; Carrey came out unscathed as well. The symbolic parallels within that movie (*The Mask*, if you didn't already know) to what I'm talking about are many.

Next, I want to move to a lesser-known term and phenomenon (and therefore probably new to you), which I learned from Ken Wilber and have since developed my own experience and understanding of, called the *subpersonality*.

Subpersonality

Have you ever been going about a usual day, having a pretty good day as a matter of fact, when suddenly something unexpected, seemingly minuscule (or at least seen by another as normal or neutral), happens that sends you into a tailspin of emotion, "running stories," and unwanted mental suffering? An innocent glance from your partner, or someone cuts you off while driving, or something you see on the news or in a movie, or a casual request from a co-worker? A chain of reactivity sends shockwaves through your system, and it feels as though another "you" takes over your whole body-mind complex! It may last a few minutes or a few hours, but even after the initial intensity, there are still remnants of the event; feelings and thoughts processing through. You shake it off, come to your senses, realizing you overreacted, apologize (if you acted in a way that warrants apology) and say, "I don't know what came over me!" Sound familiar? Of course it does!

Unfortunately this scenario is all too familiar to all of us. What did come over you? Why did you react that way? Why did it seem completely out of your control? Why did you end up doing or saying something you regret, whether mild or severe? Well, let me introduce you to a concept (and a self that you need to know about) called subpersonality.[97] Just knowing about its (or their) existence, function, and m.o. (just like knowing the ego's) is likely to give you a different perspective from which to respond more level-headedly the next time a situation like the above arises. If, as we've seen, the *personality* is the primary mask we wear, the *subpersonality* is a mask (or masks) beneath the mask (hence the prefix "sub"). If this starts to sound a little like schizophrenia or multiple personality disorder, it's not altogether different (just perhaps without the clinical diagnosis)—don't you feel a little fractured sometimes, with no control over who's running the show? There are, in fact, potentially many, many subpersonalities depending on multiple factors: how much interior work you've done, how traumatic or dramatic your life experience has been, how unprocessed your nexus-knots/samskaras are, how strong the ego's grip is, how unconscious or unaware you are to your own behavior and thinking patterns, how willing or unwilling you are to take responsibility for your own healing and liberation (à la the Basic presented in our last chapter) to name a few.

So how does a subpersonality form? Remember the nexus-knots from the Meditation Practice chapter—Whenever a particularly traumatic (perceived negative) or dramatic (perceived positive) event occurs that is not fully processed through all layers of the system (remember the koshas?) and in-real-time let go of, a nexus-knot is formed. If you can stay on top of your work, remain neutral, and observe the process without getting too emotionally involved while the wound is healed up, then the chances of a subpersonality are less. But if you are not already privy to the wiles of the ego, the new knot is a perfect host site for it schemes. It will approach the area psycho-soma-spiritually, and thus pitch a story about *how awful* or *how wonderful* the situation is. And if there's a part of yourself that's caught up in the trauma or drama, not participating in the healing process, it will likely bite the bait and fragment itself off even further. If the story is *how awful*, then a subpersonality forms, dictated by the ego, whose job is to manipulate the world so that that thing never happens again...or pushes hard against any remnant reminder of the hurt. If the story is *how wonderful*, then a subpersonality forms, dictated by the ego, whose job is to manipulate the world so that that thing always happens...or clings so that whatever-it-is never goes away (the character Gollum in *The Lord of the Rings* and his "Precious" is a perfect example).

And any time the same scenario plays out, or a similar scenario that reminds the subpersonality of "what happened last time," and reproduces a similar *feeling* throughout the body-mind (again, either desired or shunned), it will "act out" accordingly to reinforce and be validated for its existence as given its meaning by either pain or pleasure. Ken says that subpersonalities are formed along the normal developmental growth trajectory of a human, and are particularly found at the main chakras—i.e., e.g., if a baby is not fed appropriately by their mother, they may develop a subpersonality around the 1st chakra that continues on into adulthood and which is characterized by overwhelming, insatiable cravings for sustenance, and if severe enough, will turn into an eating disorder coupled with an intense fear of not being taken care of. Or a child who is *overly* nurtured and coddled emotionally can become an addict of the 2nd chakra sensation of affection, confuse it with love, and as an adult have either an unnatural, co-dependent relationship with the parent, or a sexual obsession with others exhibiting the same doting interest.

While the subpersonality is certainly *part* of the primary personality, it's mostly incognito until it gets triggered. But when it gets triggered, it's a monstrous inner demon that seems to paralyze and possess the otherwise calm and collected face mask presented to the outside. Typically, the primary persona acts as an outer shell with two agendas: to keep the exterior world out and keep the hidden interior stuff hidden. It can be a functional, practical, and useful filter as well as a calloused, in-denial defense mechanism. The subpersonalities in all their glory usually come out "behind closed doors" anyway, with those we claim to love the most; strange huh? Now, of course, that's not to say some of our most public figures (be they politicians, rock stars, or actors) are not acting from an incredibly wounded and over-compensatory place trying to fill a void of attention or fame or power or control or money. But what I am saying is that, unfortunately, those very ones, in my opinion, are operating from the very best the *primary personality* can do, and that there are even deeper and darker *subpersonalities* lurking beneath the surface in them! Technically speaking, I am simply distinguishing between the personality and the subpersonalities. Even the stereotypical masks of the public sphere—the staunch stoicism of a presiding judge, the hard edge of a cop on the streets, the smiles and glam of a movie star—are both motivated by and trying to conceal something far more threatening, menacing, and frightening (to them and everyone else) hiding in the shadows; and which more than likely comes out when the world isn't watching.

A subpersonality that was deeply embedded in me for years (the largest majority of which has been uprooted through this work) was what we might call the Guilty One. Born in the crossfire of a Church that told me I was a sinner, the same legalism that gave me a set of rules to follow but told me if I ever successfully followed them I was being arrogant and no longer in the Jesus Club, an obsessive-compulsive brain that had scrupulosity as an overarching symptom, and a poorly guided puberty in regards to sexual expression and suppression, the Guilty One, fed by the ego, was a goblin of a problem, reinforced itself by a barrage of badness. As a note to remember, and thus the point I'm trying to make: it wanted to stay very discreet, for no one to know, because obviously this was not my primary personality nor the way I presented myself to the world; but was enacted in the dark, in sneaking and secrecy (though I cried out for help in public forums, "confessing" my sins and admitting what I'd done, though no one could hear me).

My dial has been tuned for full-on healing and liberation since I was a child, and my willingness to go through the fire, I believe, was seen and rewarded. This particular nexus-knot wove a tangled web of suffering and heaviness and seeming inescapability until not only did my hard work and dedication eventually pay off, but I had a key realization that made all the difference: In the holographic understanding of reality (and remember the consideration of benevolent projection from the Taking Responsibility chapter—i.e., the Heavenly Father Hologram *wants* you to see yourself, so It allows you to project all your "stuff" at a manageable arm's length so it can be reflected back and owned) I realized that this subpersonality was actually pulling the strings and manipulating "me" to create situations that were in fact my fault, in which I did indeed say and do things I shouldn't have and never would again (as though under some kind of spell), and in which my own (mis)perceived guilt was reflected back (by an "other" being upset with me, for example, along with physical symptoms as well: sour pit in my stomach, cold sweats, hot flashes...), and the ego, or the Guilty One could whisper in my ear, "See, you *are* bad." How twisted. But that's how it works in this hall of mirrors, and that's how it happened for me.

So, again, with the combination of everything, the implementation of all the Basics, and of course the grace of God, I began recognizing those instances where there was a *need* to feel guilty and be punished, and sort of rewrote my own program: Knowing the behavior was only the final manifestation of the deeply rooted belief, I was finally free from acting out! If I started to feel guilt, I short-circuited the mechanism that would eventually *make* someone else punish me by meditating, sitting with the *feeling* without the interpreted *meaning*, turning to Ultimate I Am-ness, knowing that I am not bad or wrong, and remembering that everything is arising in My Awareness (orchestrated *for me*), including this entire self-perpetuating loop—and finally it stopped. There are traces here and there, but I know how to handle them now, and I know it's simply the bug leaving the system. Mostly there is a lightness and ease where the choke hold used to be, and an awakeness that was hypnotized by lies. *El diablo*, the ol' Opponent, my challenger still tests, and attempts to use other nexus-knots for its platform, but the momentum of Good has overridden the Bad, the interior muscles have strengthened, and my pass rate is much, much higher.

Stages of Consciousness

As I've already said, it would be greatly beneficial to your under-standing and assimilation of everything I teach if you had a basic grasp of Ken Wilber's Integral framework.[98] If you don't specifically read or study it verbatim, of course you will get it vicariously simply by absorb-ing mine. However, I would like for you to have a conscious cognition of what he calls *stages* of consciousness (particularly on the interior, as that's what concerns us here). For me to give a comprehensive-enough overview, it would probably overshadow the rest of the material in this book (it's *that* important)—contrary to its omission indicating lack of importance, its omission is due to its implication in everything I say. One day, probably in the 2.0 version of this book, I will more explicitly roll out my own transcended and included theory of Ken's stages (which in-troduces a concept called *Octaves*). With all of that said, I would strongly encourage you to watch my 4-part video series on the website, very conspicuously called *Stages 1*, *Stages 2*, *Stages 3*, and *Stages 4*, and scan over the following table. Ken has his own table that gives a graphic rep-resentation, and there is certainly overlap between the two; but please know, I did not copy nor directly reference his (though his is profoundly "integrated" into my being, and I rely heavily on some of the words he uses)—all of this is straight off the top of my head. Suffice it to say for now that the reason this is included in the Who Am I? chapter is that the *relative* self, in addition to experiencing and being expressed as a per-sonality, or fractured subpersonalities, or ego "I," or meditative states of consciousness, also grows through predictable grooves of develop-ment called *stages*. One more quick note: Integral is at the top of the chart which indicates it is higher than the others, so you may want to start at the bottom, with Magic, and read your way up; also, Integral is not the highest—it's just the highest that the average population should be aware of for now. I have more to say about what's above Integral in my videos, and most likely in *Kaliana Way 2.0*.

Level	Cognitive	Cultural	Moral	Self	Spiritual
Integral	• "2nd tier" • multi-perspective (honors and contextualizes all previous perspectives) • comprehensive • first to recognize benefit and necessity of all previous • integrates best of all • looks for a meta-map, meta-theory • limitations (what to transcend): removed from direct experience and seeing; conjecture and theory based; states of consciousness separate and filtered through stage still; may or may not utilize transcendent states • strengths (what to include): ALL	• conveyor belt	• discernment in context with multi-layer understanding	• self-boundary includes me + us + them + everyone + "thy enemies" + all previous	• multi-level God/Spirit • sees all religions have multiple levels -free to pick and choose and "integrate" with discernment • -not all saying the "same" thing; but all saying something valuable
Pluralistic	• non-marginalizing • 4 perspectives (me + us + them + everyone) • not black and white • post-modern art, etc. • breakdown, deconstruct all structures • inclusive • limitations (what to transcend): usually marginalizes all lower levels in attempt to not marginalize (inherent contradiction), "anything goes" mentality, non-judgment goes too far into non-discernment • strengths (what to include): culturally, politically, and interpersonally sensitive to many different viewpoints	• melting pot • everyone has a voice • freedom and liberation movements (women, civil, gay rights, etc) • multicultural	• no one right way • locally specific • all ways are right	• self-boundary includes "all of us"	• "spiritual not religious" • likes the word "Universe" not "God" • all paths lead to same • New Age movement • multi-myth (all saying same thing)

Rational	• dawn of logic and reason • "think about it" • not just because you told me or I have to make my own decisions • 3 perspectives (me + group + "other" outside my group even if mine is still best) • individualistic (what works for me) • mathematically 2+2 • limitations (what to transcend): have to have logical proof, God is not logical, so can get stuck spiritually thinking God is only pre-rational, judgment against pre-rational, often sacred is lost • strengths (what to include): finally considers perspective of "other" groups, deconstructs fairy tales, doesn't blindly believe, doesn't have to buy into myth of family, nation, religion, fairy tale God dismantled • -personal freedom	• secular, "worldly" • philosophy that makes sense	• right way for me • do what I want • can't tell me what to do	• world centric • self-boundary includes anyone that is "thinking rationally"	• God that makes sense to me • see for myself, see to believe • considers and allows "other" religions, even if mine is still best • often God becomes more of an idea, a principle • higher power is Intellect and Reason • not sure if all paths lead to same, but ok with other paths existing • breaks away from dominance of myth and authority
Mythic	• belief based • 2 perspectives (me + others in my group) • dogmatic • membership oriented, around the myth, story, principles • limitations (what to transcend): marginalizes the "other," not rational, my group right or wrong, have to give away power to authority • strengths (what to include): transcends ego only to include others in my group, cohesive, commitment "no matter what"	• nation, family, religion, cult • you're either in or out • orthodoxy	• set tenets to follow, usually "given" by a higher power	• ethnocentric • self-boundary includes more than just myself	• faithful to "our" God • judgmental toward other religions • mono-myth, given and fixed for all times • conversion emphasis
Magic	• superstitious • I perspective (me) • fairy tale • Santa Claus • imaginative • limitations (what to transcend): not rational, unquestioned, self-protective, not belonging to a group, "selfish" • strengths (what to include): connects to an "other world," communicates with higher power, even if superstitiously	• tribal (no others") • enmeshed oneness	• kill or be killed • dog eat dog • self-preservation • attack and protect • look out for #1	• egocentric • me vs. everyone	• fairy tale God • magical • unquestioned • karma (and favor of divine) as punish/reward

How to grow/Concepts to remember

• Take the perspective of as many "others" as possible	• Find ways to be more inclusive AND more discerning
• Try on the lens of the positive attributes of the stage just above you	• Utilize the best of reason, faith, AND spiritual intelligence
• "Transcend and include" (let go of limitations of current stage, implement strengths into next)	• Actual growth, taking root, not mere flashes and cognitive understanding only
• Make the subject, object (the subject of one stage becomes the object of the subject of the next)	• All best of all previous SHOULD be included (distort and abort if not)
• Meditate, stimulate cognition (cognition is "necessary, not sufficient"-KW)	• Even if less than Integral, understand now that ALL stages are important
	• If you can "see it" it's beneath you; if you can't, it's "over your head" and a growing edge
• Marinate in understanding of stages (self-activating)	• Birth of new stage requires death of old

Ultimate Self Identity

So, who are you? Well, you are all of the above and none of the above. The perspective is what matters. By now you're getting the hang of Ultimate vs relative, and if you've already read the Ultimates chapter, then you should have no trouble extrapolating the information found there to what we're talking about here. *If it doesn't change it's Ultimate; if it changes it's relative. The only change the Ultimate has is in its relative experience of It (but technically, the Ultimate is not experienceable).* You now know the consequences of attaching to or over-identifying with anything relative, or giving ultimate meaning to something relative, or relating with the Ultimate from a relative place, or assuming you've found the Ultimate when it's merely a profound relative—for *if it's relative, you simply are not that...ultimately...and the Ultimate is all there is.*

The process of dislodging the center of gravity identity from an illusory relative is called *dis-identification*. It's an interior muscle that requires practice to cultivate if you do it willingly, as well as a painful prying of your hands, so to speak, if unwillingly. As with any spiritual truth, the ego can take hold of it and twist it to fit its needs. In the case of dis-identifying, it can go too far into denial or pathological dissociation. In healthy disidentification, you simply let go of your current grasp of, or identity with, that which is relative, changing, being asked of you to surrender, or something that in a flash of realization you know clearly *I am not that.* It may be all in an instant, in a Satori type experience, which itself requires a period of integration; or it could be slow and steady, like a child's independency from its mother and the mother's role as primary nurturer. Any role that is played beyond the natural arch of its existence, or clung to past its maturation, or over-identified with when its no longer relevant is a prime candidate for disidentification.

The Ultimate question Who Am I?, then, is answered with the basic injunction *Who's the you that's never changed among all the you's that have?* And as with all Ultimates, there is no answer that can be said outright. The answer is the shift in consciousness itself, and "who you are," when you ask the question and follow the prompting. As I see it, of all the Ultimates that I have identified in this book, the ones concerning Who I Am (in a directly perceivable fashion) are all of the 1st person perspectives, namely Witness, I Am-ness, Self, and maybe Presence.

You know the "sense of self" that has been the steady, constant stream your whole entire life? The I that you were before you had a name? The one essence that has never changed through all the changes? That which has been and is aware of every thing "you" have ever experienced? The one behind the one reading these words? The one looking through the one looking through your eyes? Who sees all, yet cannot be seen? Who is the Unchanging Witness that watches all things come and go but Itself does not come or go? Who is the I that animates a body? Who is wearing all masks but Itself is not a mask? Who is the Unwavering Self that is behind the self tossed by the waves of the world? Who is the One aware of all personalities, all little-me's, and the ego but is not identified with any of them? When the plug is irrevocably pulled from the relative sense of self-identity, Who Are You then? I'll leave it there for now. The inquiry is endless, and if you follow it diligently, it will lead you to freedom.

The trick to every Ultimate is that you have never not known it. It's the most obvious awareness in awareness. It's too obvious to miss, and yet so obvious every person misses it until something taps them on the shoulder and reminds them to look again and find that which they have always been. Everyone has to get lost in the role first; that's part of the game of this place. And, what's more, most teachers with an eye for developmental evolution of psycho-spiritual interior consciousness, say (and I would agree) you must "know thyself" as a relative self, and <u>do your work</u> to become the most mature version of that self *before and simultaneous to* transcending that self altogether. Hear this, as a principle throughout this book and all that I teach: You must first have meaning before transcending meaning. You must first be a self before being no-self. You must first construct before you deconstruct before you reconstruct. Who are you? As Rumi says, "You are the soul, of the soul, of the soul."[99] Or as I would say, you are that which is aware of that which is aware of that which is aware... The who-aware-of-whom. You!

The Third I

Some teachers, students, and even whole traditions of this work approach the identity question (i.e., Who am I?) a bit too dualistically. As you can see, my understanding, experience, and conveyance is multi-dimensional and trans-dualistic.[100] What I mean is, based on limited or low-level development, it is seen and concluded all too starkly that I am NOT the relative self whatsoever; I am That Which is aware of the relative self. Meanwhile, room is not made for any gray area, and often these folks are quite resistant to engaging the shadow aspects of the personality, so the disidentification hatch is an easy, albeit pre-mature, immature escape route; but the relative self identity lurks still in the background, wreaking sometimes more havoc than before, when it was out in the open. On another hand, some teachers, students, and traditions, particularly in the more pseudo-spiritual New Age circles, have never even considered anything beyond the conventional, relative self (therefore they don't call it that, because, well, conventional and relative compared to what? It's just me!), and they spent all their time and money and energy on "self-improvement" workshops and books and classes, and are highly identified, and absorbed, with themselves as a persona.[101]

I promote both simultaneously. That's why both and all are included in this book of Basics. As I've seen it, there are traditionally two basic ways to guide "seekers" or initiates or practitioners: One is to start with the Ultimate, and then *from there* work with the relative; one is to start with the relative, and *build up to* the Ultimate. In my opinion, both have benefits and potential pitfalls. If you start with the Ultimate, and that seeing is deep and profound enough, it puts everything in appropriate perspective, and relative objects are seen as not lasting, not reliable sources of happiness or identity, etc.; but there can develop a pathology and an aversion to anything relative (but, of course, one cannot and will not ever be able to successfully avoid the relative, no matter how anchored in the Absolute), and one may not ever "get back around to" working with the finite world, which in fact is infused with and by the Ultimate, because the Ultimate transcendent is so sweet and sublime and, well, transcendent. If you start with the relative, however, there can be a necessary conviction and commitment to "doing the work" on the shadow, the ego, what-have-you, and even a beautiful relationship with "this-worldly things," but an over-identification will almost certainly ensue, and attachment to changefulness (which has to be let go of entirely if one is to make the jump) becomes the obstacle to ever leaping into the Abyss of the Ultimate. So, as I'm saying, I prescribe an *all at once* approach to the Five Basics.

Besides the Ultimate I and the relative I, there is a third I that I can spot. The further required hair-splitting for the inevitable questions that will arise here will come in person, in videos, and in subsequent books. So don't worry. At the tippy-top of subtleties, and impossible language about that of which cannot be spoken, there is a catapult beyond the Ultimates themselves and into complete and utter Emptiness

Itself (as some kind of trans-Ultimate). In any case, the third I I would call the Nondual I. On the one hand, so far, Nonduality has itself been one of the multiple shades of Ultimate. Now I'm using it (until a more appropriate placeholder is found) as a higher I than both relative and Ultimate. It's the clear and direct seeing that I am simultaneously all relative selves at once as well as That Which Is Aware of all relative selves but is Itself not any of the relative selves (both both and and).

The Simulated Self

One more consideration (for now) regarding the question *Who am I?*, from the perspective and possibility that this entire experience could be a fractal holographic computer simulated reality, and tying back together our conversation about illusion (or what is real) and relative and Ultimate self. For as long as humans have been self-reflexive, curious, contemplative beings, we have been asking the fundamental questions, *What is this place?*, *Where are we?*, *Where did we come from?*, *How did we get here?*, *Where are we going?* These questions themselves seem as natural as breathing for us—some unnamed force in us drives us to know—and some take them more seriously than others into research endeavors and a career that supports the search, but all are innately affected by them in one way or another.

From a phenomenological perspective, i.e., first-hand direct experience rather than third-person historical theoretical conjecture, the Buddha would call this an "open question," namely, a question that has no answer, but rather has the power to liberate merely by asking and sitting with no-answer. For there truly is no answer, even in historical conjecture. We get at some speculation, and feel we're making headway, based on carbon dating and archaeology and ancient writings and astronomy, and then a groundbreaking new discovery appears that rattles the whole foundation of our previous presumption. If you simply stop, right where you are, take your mind back, slow down your thinking process, turn it in on *what is*...rather than taking for granted that anything is in the first place; for it needn't've been, and yet it is...[102]you'll inevitably come to the sneaking suspicion that something's up here. We have romanticized assumptions about past civilizations like Atlantis or tribal natives or Egyptian initiatory cultures who knew with certainty the answer to some of the questions that for us are only hazy guesses. I believe they were using what knowledge and best-guesses they had as well, just like we're doing. It still is a chasm of unknown. There is a blacker than black curtain preventing your memory from penetrating the deep recesses of the past, before your birth.[103] And there's a blacker than black curtain preventing total certainty about the future and who's pulling the strings and is anybody in charge behind the scenes.

Once, in a particularly profound meditative state (and this is documented in my journal), I had an unmistakable feeling as though the very walls around me, the floor beneath me, even the very space and air in front of my face, were all a part of "My Body," breathing with me, as me, feeling with me, as me, and a strange inclincation to take a bite out of it and see if I would feel it too—to bite the walls and feel them as flesh; to chew the space between the things in my room and see if a hole was made to the next dimension; and for the rest of the day I walked softly on the hardwood floor of my being, breathed the breeze and felt the rays of my summer skin...feeling and knowing it to be made of the same "stuff" I am, as sentient as me, as sensitive as Me.

Each and every person who has ever seriously attempted an answer—with as little preconceived bias or belief, whether scientific or religious, as possible—has come up with a very similar, but filtered through their own language, images, examples, and analogies conclusion: namely, "this place" (i.e., the third-dimensional-human, planet-Earth-realm experience) is temporary, is "not our home," (in other words somehow we don't belong here *ultimately*, and we won't be staying here "forever"). It seems universally conclusive that we ourselves are but a blip on the radar of eternity on a tiny speck of infinity, and there is a place (a planet? a state of being? an enlightened consciousness? a so-called heaven?) much greater than what we can now perceive.[104] But whether we are referring to another place among places or a transcendent state of being depends, among other things, on the relative vs Ultimate distinction, which is one obvious reason this is important to our current topic.

Currently, at the time of the publication of this first edition, we are steeped in the rapidly accelerating and evolving Age of Computer Technology and Artificial Intelligence. We no longer know our world without it, and to use an analogy, it is to music and movies as water is to a fish (i.e., we breathe it and reference it and swim in it without even knowing it). In 1999, *The Matrix* changed our paradigm forever,[105] and whether you have seen it or not (if not, I would highly recommend it), its worldview and milieu influences the way you think whether you know it or not. I won't give the synopsis here, so watch it if necessary, but "the Matrix" is now a household term to refer to the illusory world mentioned above.

In addition, not only the arts and movies, but many other fields have given us some quite compelling and provocative new concepts to consider, which are already imbued in our collective psyche, refashioning our understanding of "reality," whether we like it or not. I am thinking in particular of video games, computer simulation, "virtual reality," and the theory and prediction of the Technological Singularity put forth by Ray Kurzweil. Kurzweil and other transhumanists hold that computers are currently evolving at such an exponentially accelerated rate that eventually, in the not so distant future in fact, they will be more powerful than humans (in terms of information processing and potentially physical strength), even more cognitively intelligent than the humans that built and programmed them, and have the innate ability to transcend (and destroy) biological life altogether, making the premise of *The Matrix* movies and other "sci-fi" movies a reality.[106] In addition, Nick Bostrom's simulation theory is a compelling proposition that, because *we* are developing simulated reality experiences (for fun, for video games, and for pilot, military, and police training, etc.) that are less and less distinguishable from "real life," how do we know that what we call "real life" is not just that—a simulated reality created by either the advanced machines mentioned above or some other race of beings?[107] It's really not so far-fetched. In fact, they are planning on making the next Sims video game run by Artificial Intelligence. Think on that!

Combine the Wachowskis' concepts with Kurzweil's and Bostrom's theories (which, interestingly enough, are not merely from one field, but span art, science, and philosophy) and you have the possibility that an Intelligence beyond ours evolved to produce a simulation in which we were born, believing it to be "real," and that the Big Bang was simply when the power button as it were was pressed for the first time, booting us up. Again, not so far-fetched—even back in the day, Isaac Newton and René Descartes (again, science *and* philosophy) subscribed to the idea of the Watchmaker God; i.e., "God" made the world, wound it up, and stepped back to watch it tick itself down to nothing.

To me, these theories are merely icing on the cake of the radically inescapable "God question"—*okay, but where did that come from? Why is there something rather than nothing? Who's behind the curtain that's behind the curtain that's behind the curtain?* That's far-out (and at the same time, of course, the only thing we know and the one thing we most take for granted—existence itself!) . Everything else is just a representational explanation. I for one am not attached to any way being "<u>the</u> way it is," (because it changes, like all relatives) and does indeed require *belief* (even if not a belief in a fairy tale myth), for no one knows for sure. But it does utilize our current scientific understanding mixed with our contemporary imagination, and paints a pretty convincing picture.

Regardless, the questions remain. *What is this place? Where are we? Who are we? Where did we come from? How did we get here? Where are we going?* Think about one more consideration from this which will bring us back around to why we're talking about this in the first place. You're playing a first person-perspective "RPG"[108] video game, in which you control your character "from behind," and see the back of their head and shoulders, or sometimes their whole body, or sometimes even *through their eyes* (you've all seen this, yes?). Well, *you* know that you're in your living room and that it's "just a game," but does your character know it's just a game, know they are in a computer simulated reality? *From the character's perspective,* they are interacting with that world as though it's "real," and you (we might say the "higher self" of the character) are telling it what to do, where to go. Sometimes you may even "get lost" in the game, spend more time than you had planned playing, and become emotionally attached to your success or failure, winning or losing. But (except in extreme cases of psychotic breaks) you never really forget what's really real, and you turn the game off and go on to "real life." When you press the power button at the beginning, do you think your character (phenomenologically speaking) knows how they got there? Do they know there's a you behind them if they just turn around? Could they even turn around to look at you? Are you the back of the back of their awareness? Can they autonomously do anything at all without you?

What if that's what's happening with us?[109] We are using digital age analogies and illustrations, of course, but people have been coming to the same conclusions ever since whoever pressed whatever power button or wound the clock at the "beginning of time." Even the Hindu concept of *lila,* which is the Sanskrit word for "play" or "sport" or "drama," is the very word used to describe life. The first Hindu to use the word lila to describe this place and this human experience knew what they were saying; they just didn't have video games or *The Matrix* or technological singularity or computer simulations; but they were no doubt saying the same thing. Regardless of what images you use, the questions remain, and the blow-your-mind miracle that *something, anything,* exists at all rather than nothing, is enough to stop you in your tracks and stand in awe and wonder—with no need for explanation.

In my experience, when I am tuning into Ultimate I Am-ness, or the Ultimate Witness, or asking the Ultimate question, Who Am I?, using the only injunction(s) appropriate for such an inquiry—*if it has a beginning and end in time and space, I am not that;* and *if I can observe, feel, see, witness, notice, experience, it, I am not that*—and if I continue that movement back and back and back, as it were,[110] behind all phenomena and all relatives, I find that there is both an infinite number (on the relative-verging-on-absolute spectrum) of "things" and I's *that*

I am not, or of observable layers behind which I Am, as well as an immediate Presence of this Witness (which you are too!), that has been silently watching every thing from the beginning of time and beyond, Itself existing beyond time and space—yet intimately connected *with* time and space. And in my (as Kemper) experience of this (because every Ultimate is experienced by a finite and interpreted through that finite filter until the finite filter expands and grows enough to become One with the infinite...), there is eventually, at the way back back of awareness, an undeniable feeling, almost a manifest sensation in fact, where I come to, or hit, or knock up against a wall of awareness, the curtain behind which I cannot see, the dial tone at the end of a call, the gray static on the old TVs after the show...in a not so different way from the back of the video game character's head is right in front of the TV screen. Whoa.

But I'll take ya one step further. Is there any separation between *your* awareness as the one playing the game, or your thumbs moving on the controller, and the movements and mind of the character? Is there any separation between the back of the character's head and body and the TV screen? Is there? And now translate and extrapolate this analogy into "real life": is there any separation between your awareness and the words you are reading now? Where, oh where, are the words arising? None other than your awareness. Where, oh where, are your thoughts about the words arising? None other than your awareness. Where, oh where, is the book arising? None other than your awareness. Slow it down. Feel into it. Don't rush ahead. Now check this one out. Where, oh where, is your sense of self arising; your sense of "I"? None other than your awareness, and the very same place all these others are arising. Is it not true? And here's one to cook your noodle: Is there any separation whatsoever, from the perspective of This, between the words, and thoughts, and the book, and your self? Can you draw a line, from the perspective of the Ultimate (<u>not the relative</u>), where a thought ends and you begin? Where this book ends and you begin? Where awareness ends and your sense of "I" begins? Or me? Or you? Or me writing this to you from the past into the future? Any of it whatsoever? Have you hit the proverbial TV screen yet? Ready to crawl out of it like the girl in the movie and meet your maker, meet your higher self, meet your controller? It's ready to be found.

Another way that I experience the shiftover from Ultimate Witness or I Am-ness, inside of which all things are arising, to Ultimate Nonduality or Not-two-ness, where it is seen that objects arising inside of a subject, even the Ultimate Subject, is still dualistic and an illusion, is what I call the accordion slapback phenomenon. When I stretch back and back and back into the awareness behind awareness, like a rubber band stretching farther and farther and farther, it (awareness) can theoretically continue infinitely while still on the relative side (as we've seen); but eventually if it is to realize the Ultimate, it has to let go of that completely, and slap back to "just a rubber band," to "Just This." In other words, the Ultimate is not found by stretching the relative far enough. The rubber band does not discover who it is by becoming who it's not. The rubber band "ultimately" can be nothing other than itself, cannot expand beyond itself, can go nowhere outside of itself. Same as you, as your awareness.

But an important suggestion, or contribution, I'd like to make is this: I don't like the word "just." I prefer "all." In Nondual circles, it's common to have the conclusion be "just this." Just this arising, nothing else. And while that's true, in our vocabulary, "just" is kind of a downer. But the Nondualists claim that "just this" is the Ultimate Realization! And again, those who've seen it, know it is indeed an appropriate word; but the same as I said that mindfulness is not limited to the waking, physical, visual world alone, the Nondual "Thisness" is the Not-two-ness of All-That-Is-Arising *in* Awareness and Awareness *as which* All-That-Is-Arising. Therefore, it's Everything and Nothing, everything and nothing in particular! And it's also as inclusive as the relative lens it's being experienced through and as! This table has the same Nondual Thisness as angel voices as AK-47 fire. *You*, as the *person* and the *Awareness* are tasked with the responsibility of *seeing more* so that "Just This" is more than just this. Make sense? Good.

The Heavenly Father Hologram

Shifting gears slightly now, but building on the previous... As I see it, there are two types of oneness, relative and Ultimate. Unfortunately, all we have linguistically to differentiate them is a capital letter (oneness and Oneness). Relative oneness is the interrelationship between all *things*. Quantum science is irrefutably coming to this conclusion more and more. They say, especially, that once two photons come into contact with each other, they are irrevocably "entangled" and connected throughout all of time and space and all dimensions[111]

In the terms that we are using, however, this is all still "relative." My approach always begins with the Ultimate. Consciousness is singular, and there is only One, which means not One as a number among two, three, four, etc., but only One. Or, Zero without a one (as in, don't even start counting; once you have a one, you have to have a two, and so on to infinity). It's semantics, but at the same time, not "just" semantics. Though this is closer to my wheelhouse than the relative, this is still a third-person theoretical approach to the Ultimate. Phenomenologically, which, remember, means, from the direct, first-person experiential perspective, starting with not the "connectivity" of a bunch of things (i.e. relative oneness), but starting with the One-without-two-ness of Awareness Itself (accessible right now, right where you are, as the deepest and most immediate sense of Presence and Perception), as we have seen, and in a self-confirming way (as all Ultimates are), there is *no separation between Awareness and the things in awareness*. Therefore, awareness and the things in awareness are not "connected"—they are simply the same stuff! Who is aware of who is aware of who is aware of whom is aware of what?!?!?! Again, can you draw a line "connecting" where Your Awareness ends and the computer screen begins? Where Your Awareness ends and Kemper begins? Where is Kemper arising? Where is *[fill in the blank with your name]* arising? In Your Awareness, Here, Now. No?

And as Consciousness is singular, One without two, and all things within it, if you in your center of gravity, and indeed, You as the

Center of the Universe (and if this is not seen egoically, but *truly*) are identified as such, and you are not identified as your name (only), then "the whole thing" becomes alive and responsive and intelligent and intimately relatable...with yourself, as yourself. This brings an entire new meaning to prayer and the now-popular New Age "law of attraction" or manifestation theory. Jesus says, "Who of you parents, if your child asked for a fish would give them a serpent? Who of you parents, if your child asked for a piece of bread would give them a stone? How much more then will your Father Who Is In Heaven give you what you need?"[112] The problem, and the rebuttal, then becomes, "But I've been trying and asking for money and using the law of attraction to try and find a romantic partner and it's not working! Why is it not working?"

Combining quantum entanglement and law of attraction with the possibility of a computer simulated reality as well as a holographic understanding of the universe, I upgrade Jesus' terms and call it the Heavenly Father Hologram. The answer to the problem above is that probably that person is praying or asking or manifesting *from* the ego. If there is an unresolved issue around relationship or insecurity or deficiency, then the law of projection and reflection requires the Hologram to manifest back to you exactly what you are asking for even if you don't realize you're asking for it! So you will magnetize the exact thing you're trying to avoid if you're asking from an egoic identified contracted place. So the answer is: You're not asking for a piece of bread; you're actually asking for a stone, and that's why you're getting a stone! You're not asking for a fish; you're actually asking for a serpent, and that's why you're getting a serpent! You're not asking for a relationship; you're actually asking for someone to fill a void that can never be filled with another person, so that's what you're getting!

My conclusion is that the Heavenly Father Hologram *always responds, always answers prayers, always gives you what you ask for, AND what you need.* That's Its way of loving us as well as providing the means to be set free.[113] It is not only highly intelligent, but also highly Benevolent. Therefore, when you get what you think you don't want or didn't ask for, that's the opportunity to do the deeper work around *who's* actually asking; *what* you're actually asking for! To "do the work" to dismantle the ego that's asking from a contracted, deficient place, as well as to identify from a place of (Ultimate) Oneness "with" All That Is, and with the Heavenly Father Hologram Itself (hence Jesus can say "I and the Father are One" and "I do nothing that I do not see the Father doing" and "The Father will give you anything you ask for in my name"[114]—"my name" meaning something like Christ Consciousness, not a Magic/Mythic understanding of Jesus).

Once this has happened, then you don't *have* to ask for anything because your will and the will of the All is Already One! There is no separation between what you want and what you have! God's will *is* your will; your will *is* God's will. This is also not a lowly evolved understanding resulting in resignation or "putting up with" or "dealing with" whatever you're given even if you don't want it. It's seen that you want what you have, that you have what you want, that you're given what you ask for, that you're asking for what you're being given. And it all comes down to *who's* asking, and perhaps *why?* Is it you as an illusory ego contraction, or You as the singular point of consciousness that is the Center of the Universe and not separate from the Heavenly Father Hologram? And is it because you think you *need* something, or profoundly because you are at one with the perfect unfolding of your path and everything is already provided?

And therefore, beyond the "every *thing* is connected" understanding in third-person scientific/mathematical terms, All is Already One, Intelligent, Responsive, Intimate, Benevolent, and none other than Your Self Here, Now. So, what is this place? Where are we (going)? We may never know from an analytical, third-person, theoretical perspective. But the invitation has always been to do the work necessary to be free of the illusion while at the same time learning how to work with it while it's here, and discovering Who You Are Now and Now and Now.....

Interior Domain

———— ♦ ————

As you can see, I rely heavily on my study and understanding of Ken Wilber's brilliantly pioneering work. There are some vocabulary words and concepts that he established, or extended from others himself, that are simply here to stay (until something better comes along). There are already many ways that I "transcend and include"[115] Ken's model.[116] One set of vocabulary words, in addition to *transcend and include* and others, that I am faithful to is his use of *interior* vs *exterior*. The interior is the world of feelings, symbols, interpretation, texture, and mind (what he calls the Lefthand Quadrants). The exterior is the world of observation, measurement, sensory organs, and brainwave patterns (what he calls the Righthand Quadrants). The exterior is not merely the physical visual gross waking world—the physical visual gross waking world has exterior as well as interior components (i.e., what an apple tastes like is interior; what an apple looks like is exterior. What the sun feels like is interior; how hot the sun is is exterior).

Most of our educational conditioning, throughout all of standardized schooling, prioritizes the exterior,[117] which is one reason we mistake it as the "real" world and are usually very underdeveloped or completely cut off from the interior altogether. We are taught how to ride a bike. We are not taught how to consciously be in the present moment.[118] We are taught how to type on a keyboard. We are not taught how to take responsibility for projections. We are taught how to brush our teeth. We are not taught how to meditate. We are taught how to throw a ball. We are not taught how to let go of a destructive thought pattern or what it means to not cling to *things*. We are taught how to write in cursive. We are not taught how to understand why we feel certain intense emotions and what to do with them. We are taught how to cook dinner for ourselves. We are not taught how to disidentify from a contracted ego-identity or grow from immature subpersonalities to mature versions of our unique personality. We are taught to play kickball and hide-and-seek. We are not taught to concentrate the mind on a single point of focus until it is tripped into a transcendent state of Oneness. Luckily, some alternative schools are indeed exploring this interior training, starting in kindergarten; but my generation, and the generations just before mine, largely did not, and the majority still do not; and even still, the ones that are now getting their toes wet in such waters have a long way to go. We have to start somewhere, though, yeah?[119]

In addition to the commitment and dedication to wading through the muck before the clearing happens, it requires quite a bit of training of the interior muscles, which, in my opinion and experience, are just as "real" as our exterior muscles, but are sorely underdeveloped (and that's an understatement). Just as important (and I might argue *more* important) as the ability to move the physical, exterior body through time and space, or the automatic response of turning the head to the command, "Look over here," or to knowing *where* to look when a finger is pointed in a particular direction, or to reaching down to pick up an object when a friend says, "Can you hand me that?," or to open the hand when someone says, "Let go!" is the ability to "look," with interior muscles into specific landscapes and spaces pointed to on the *interior* (like the Causal realm, or the ability to describe what a thought *feels* like) or to "let go" of an attachment, or to, on command drop into the Present Moment or "hold onto" a thread of contemplation to completion.

As children, we are conditioned to prioritize the exterior world as the "real" world, and more detrimental than making the interior secondarily real, we are cut off from it entirely, or are even taught that "imagination" means *not real*; when in fact, the imagination is the interior place where *images* are formed and held, and *from which* the projector projects that image out onto the exterior world to reflect back an object and interpreted through as an idea. The imagination is closer to where reality begins than the object we blindly take to be real! We are taught to identify *red truck* and *blue sky* and *A is for Apple* and *B is for Boy*, and this is a cat and this is a dog, but not to identify interior sources of suffering or what the Theta brainwave zone feels like and what is experienced there. These are real. And they are interior. And the interior is what this entire book has been about.

Yoga

With that, I'd like to take an important side trail and mention the one exterior component that is, from my perspective, absolutely vital to all that I've mentioned thus far (but that, in its very nature, is a deeply interior practice)—Yoga. Just like the *stages* conversation, the fact that it's largely omitted from the rest of the book is actually because it's *implied* and *assumed* in everything I say, is on the highly important end of the importance spectrum, and is so important that it would take up too much space here were I to give it adequate attention. Indeed, I don't know "the work" without Yoga.

Unfortunately, there is also a theme in the Western yoga world similar to the one we find in the Pluralistic New Age culture (my opinion about which I have made clear enough): i.e., the originally discovered and intended depth in the interior traditions has been bastardized by our ego-driven, achievement-oriented, surface-level neuroses; and yoga has in large part become synonymous with a mere fitness class, or has been squeezed into a physical practice only (when all the ancient texts clearly hold the physical to be only a small part, leading to and supporting a deep contemplation of the divine), or is causing injuries rather than healing them, or is tainted by wannabe gurus who drag their students and communities through selfish scandals over money, power, and sex.

I myself have had first-hand experience and encounters with not a few instances of each of these shameful scenarios. I have rubbed shoulders with many so-called yoga celebrities, have been a privileged manager at one of the largest yoga conglomerates in the country which has since lost its momentum and the respect of the collective due to the very things listed above, and have injured myself *in yoga class* from lack of appropriate training by instructors.

Alas, as with all that I'm saying in this book, grace abounds, and if the path is authentic, and the willingness genuine, you will find yourself on the good and true, or it will find you, and the depraved human ingredients will quickly pale in the light guiding your way. Such is what has happened with me, and I have learned many lessons which I now incorporate into the way I deliver (and practice) Yoga as I believe it was meant to be. Of course, as always, I am not going to pretend I know *exactly* how the original Yogis intended it in the caves (or how "the gods" came down and presented it to them) thousands of years ago; and I do desire to honor what was while taking into consideration what's now. What I do know is that *Yoga*, in fact, has an almost identical etymological connotation to *religion*—"to unite," or "bind," or "connect." Why has the same shallow, inauthentic, laced-with-scandal water contaminated both? Why, on the average, is neither yoga nor religion living up to their name, not doing what they're supposed to do—to bring an intimately transcendent direct experience of healing and liberation and Union with God and Self to *anyone* who takes up the path and practice?

But lest I lose you in my pontificating, I can speak to how Yoga has changed my life—in healing of body, nervous system, and psycho-energetic wounds of the past; in supplementing my removal of pharmaceuticals through the stability provided during withdrawal symptoms; in its hand-in-hand relationship with my seated meditation practice; and in connecting me to God *through* my body (i.e., transcending and including, rather than transcending *only*, sitting disembodied and detached on my cushion). Therefore it goes without saying, Yoga is an irreconcilable piece of the Basics for me, and it is a joy to deliver my little sliver of an authentic version of it to my students.

I will leave you with this, before we continue: Though *asana* (aka the physical piece of Yoga) is an exterior engagement, Yoga as a system in its wholeness is primarily concerned with the stuff of this book, namely, the cultivation of the interior life; and you can't have one without the other. So find a style of yoga that honors more than just the physical practice, that has instructors adequately trained in the therapeutic aspect and not just fitness and circus tricks, and that supports both your healing *and* liberation, with the implementation of our Five Basics in mind. If you don't know where to start, contact me through the website, and I can lead you in the right direction. If you're local, come to a class at the studio. And if you're not local, at the time of this writing, I teach a weekly online class which I would love to have you join!

Transbiological Endeavor

In many ways, the spiritual (or interior) journey is what I call a "transbiological" endeavor. Every tradition, in its esoteric version at least, invites its practitioners into a "more than merely animalistic" understanding of and relationship with "natural" functions like food, sex, sleep, violence, emotional reaction, identity, and fear, among others. Have you ever watched the docuseries *Planet Earth,*[120] *Blue Planet, Life,* or *One Strange Rock?* If not, check them out; not only for an awe-inspiring experience, and an uplifting, not-drenched-with-mindless-drama TV show, but also for quite an honest and close-up look at just what goes on in "nature." It's more weirder and wonderful than we ever imagined; a perspective changer, for sure. Before we had such a globalization of multi-media communication along with the ability to access, with highly advanced cameras, the darkest underground caves, the bottomless depths of the ocean, the ecosystems of the tiniest micro-microorganisms, savage plants that intelligently choke out competition, the view of the thin blue firmament from just outside the atmosphere, and the means to observe, from within, the behavior patterns of some of the most dangerous predators, I think it's safe to say scientists were just best-guessing and making grand assumptions about our fellow terrestrial travelers. But when you watch the above mentioned footage, the dual point (besides the breathtaking beauty and mind-bending bizarreness of our planet) is obvious: the world of plants and animals and rocks and dirt is not only *sentient* like we are, but it's ruthless. It's violent. It's deceptive. It's "selfish." It's reactive.

It's volatile. Don't get me wrong, it's not *only* those things, but it most certainly *is* those things. Stay with me as I make the point I'm wanting to make.

In addition to the fractalized holographic simulated reality theory I dazzled you with, there are, as you know, more than a few other paradigms that attempt to explain where we came from, who put us here, how long we've been here, and just what it means to be "human." Without making prejudiced assumptions, whether evolutionary or religious, about being "better than" or "more evolved than" or that humans are the crowning achievement of God's creation, we can all agree that humans in our current form—*homo sapiens sapiens*—are indeed uniquely *different* from other species, and even mainstream science is discovering that we are a cocktail mixture of various types of DNA. And depending on how close to the controversial edge you want to make your claims, some say apes, some say angels, some say "otherworldlies," and some say all three. Some also say there are clear moments in the history that point to deliberate tampering, or splicing, and neither on the one hand *poof-and-here-we-are*, nor on the other smooth random evolution from a single cell. It's somewhere in the middle; and doesn't it feel that way intuitively?[121] Friedrich Nietzsche said, "Humanity is a rope stretched between the animal and the superhuman."[122] Yeah, something like that. And this is found right under our nose in our most cherished religious texts; we're just typically blinded by the Magic-Mythic fairy tale belief system to really think Rationally what it could actually mean and the implications thereof. Without this fuller picture, some reduce humans to merely a sophisticated ape on the one hand, or elevate us to the superior race disconnected from Earth's web altogether on the other (hence the justified dominance of, rather than cooperation with, Gaia's system). We are, however, the "sore thumb," the fungus among an otherwise cohesively connected planet, and haven't quite figured it all out yet.

I'm getting to my transbiologcal point, I promise. Those who reduce us to sophisticated apes "only" are apt to say something like, "Without laws and government we would just return to our animalistic ways of rape and pillage and killing each other...You know, survival of the fittest, dog-eat-dog...the way "nature" is; those are our *natural* instincts." From my perspective, yes and no. Those characteristics do indeed live inside of us, but to use Ken Wilber's terminology, as a collective of human beings, our interior consciousness itself has evolved beyond that, and we have "transcended and included"[123] the qualities of our terrestrial cousins (and even if some still exist at the lower levels of interpersonal relationship and ethics, the capacity for care and love and self-transcendence beyond murder and violence and egocentrism has now been established, and is always pointed to by the sages and seers). How come animals have not evolved in such a way? This potential, it seems, if not confined to, is at least unique to, humans, and is the baseline for the next invitation for what we're concerned with here: the further evolution of interior consciousness on the "spiritual path," and beyond the biosphere entirely (in a transcendently included kind of way of course).

Every exoteric religion (or to use our term, exterior tradition) has some sort of behavioristic rule system or set of laws or tenets to follow (interestingly, almost identical across the board), which is fine enough on its own to mechanically ensure that we stay "higher than the animals," but which sadly typically ends in despair, depression, guilt, a white-knuckled approach to morality, and authoritarian control by the ones in charge. Here's my perspective about the use of the universal tenets for the interior (I did not hear this from anyone else, but perhaps someone else has come to the same conclusion, and whether it was "originally" intended this way or not, I don't know). If you think about it, each tradition has their list of rules *at the beginning*—i.e., the Ten Commandments of the Judeo-Christian world, the Noble Eightfold Path of Buddhism, and the Yamas and Niyamas of Patanjali's Yoga Sutras are among the first principles learned by newcomers. Why? Because, I believe (and this is also from my experience), in the deeper, esoteric, contemplative, interior, truly transformational versions of the paths, eventually all conditioning, as well as the practitioner's very self-identity is brought into question, deconstructed to the core, and dismantled to the point where it is clearly and directly seen that "nothing is real," that there truly is "no self," and from the Ultimate Nondual perspective (not mere Green Pluralism), that nothing is inherently good or bad, right or wrong. But here's the crux: If the bodymind is still left after that, with a few or a lot of years left to tick off the clock, and a newly reborn spirit is to re-integrate into the culture, into interpersonal relationships, into a conventional, practical life in any way, they will need to have a navigating compass—otherwise risk slipping into various possibilities of pathology: nihilism, sloth, depression, sociopathy, neurosis, you name it. Again, I know this from experience. So, I believe the ethical principles at the outset of the path are indelibly important for when that moment happens. "Good people" are not the only ones who meditate and discover Oneness, meditation doesn't automatically make "bad people" good, and really good and bad has nothing to do with the deepest waters of Ultimate Realization; let's just put it that way.[124]

To take it even a step further, however, to what we might call interior transhumanism,[125] we need to start looking at how the traditions call us to go beyond not only our animal natures, but also our conditioned "sophisticated," "civilized" moral codes and interpersonal etiquette. The contemplative Christian tradition holds in high regard the process prominently put forth by St. John of the Cross called the dark night of the soul.[126] Patanjali's Eight Limbed Path of Raja Yoga has a direct correlate, though not as thoroughly and concisely expressed as the dark night template (at least not in my research and awareness), called *Pratyahara* (translated as "withdrawal of the senses"). It's the exact same as dark night, but, again, I don't know if many folks draw the parallel as I do. In both systems, this is the inescapable prerequisite gateway before higher stages of contemplation, awakening, Union, Oneness, Yoga, Samadhi, etc. are reached. It's the eye of the needle, to use Jesus' words, or the narrow way that few find (or the "Middle Way," to use Siddhartha's[127]). Now the serious sojourner must begin shedding all attachment to all things whatsoever. The dark night process, or *Pratyahara*, can be intentionally implemented by simply and with searing honesty noticing areas in which you reach for *things* to fill a perceived void, and challenging that pattern by not only abstaining but also sitting in the empty emptiness, and the feelings that arise as a result, of not trying to fill it for once.

Especially in our privileged Euro-American white middle-to-upper-class society (and let's face it, if you're reading this book, you're probably in that category right along with me—though I pray it reaches further!), even if you're "on a budget," you can still pretty much do what you want. You can go out to eat and binge on pizza and beer, you can press a button (or touch a touchscreen; God forbid we have to *press* a button!) and binge on movies, you can slide your finger *up* the touchscreen and binge on gossip and fake newsfeeds; you can swipe left and right and binge on the outer shells of human bodies and judge if you want to go on a date with them; you can "open a new tab" and binge on cute cat videos or if you want other human bodies having sex *like* animals; you can have an emotional response to a co-worker and binge on projected hateful thoughts about them which are probably hateful thoughts about yourself anyway; you can watch Fox News (or CNN for that matter) and binge on fear porn and lies... Basically, *binge is in baby!* And ease of access doesn't mean shit; accessibility is inversely proportional to the degree to which it actually satisfies. But no-*thing* was ever meant to satisfy anyway (remember relative vs Ultimate?).

So what if one day you just didn't reach? Or for whatever reason you *can't* any longer reach—for the remote, for the snack, for the thought, for the phone, for the feel-good dopamine rush, for the story that reinforces a false sense of purpose...identity...meaning? What if for once you didn't try to escape whatever it is you're trying to escape from? I hear someone in the crowd saying, "But what's wrong with pizza and beer? But what's wrong with cute cat videos? But what's wrong with... What's wrong with... Why can't I...?" The answer is, *inherently* nothing. And even though there *is* inherent suffering in each of these temporary pleasures, that's not the place that one's coming from anyway; that one's coming from a *don't-take-my-toys-away* kick-and-scream. No one is required to take this route, however. It's just a tried-and-true route to freedom, that's all. And even if it's not a binge but an "every now and then" thing. Still, if there's a subtle avoidance, or a subtle need or clingy desire to "get" something or "add" something or fill an emptiness or find happiness with any *thing*[128] whatsoever, it will be tinged with sadness. And especially if you are reading this book and embarking on this "transbiological interior endeavor," all of it has to be let go of.

Spoiler alert! You get to receive back everything that's truly good; all you have to surrender is everything you are not. But to start, we usually don't have an appropriate grasp (no pun intended) on what's truly good, or what we are not, so the entire process must be completed before that happens. That means, don't jump ahead. That's why the Traditions have a *one-step-at-a-time grasshoppa* mentality. And what's truly good then is infused with the knowledge and experience of something greater. Happiness, fulfillment, meaning, identity in That Which cannot be taken away. This can look like many things, but primarily there must be an actual shift in seeing the relationship between attachment to things and unfulfilled, unsatisfied attempts at filling a void that no-thing can.

On the other hand, the dark night, or *Pratyahara*, can descend without your permission (but of course always requires your cooperation). It can come during a mid-life crisis, or a crisis of faith, or a crisis of health, or when something that your identity is wrapped up in is questioned, removed, revealed as untrue, or the proverbial rug is pulled out from under your unstable feet.

In any case, this is the gateway to the higher interior realms of contemplation and being in which the "basic" needs of sex, food, sleep, and emotional response are transformed. Think about our animal kingdom again in this light: Try to tell a rabbit not to be afraid; it's its nature as a preyed-upon species. Try to tell a lioness not to rip to shreds some cackling hyenas lurking after her cubs. Try to tell a male peacock not to narcissistically strut his stuff to attract a mate and get his groove on; and then in the very same season do it over and over to multiple other females. Try to tell a bluejay not to rob another bird's nest and make it its own. Try to tell a tree not to ravenously compete for the sun's nourishment while others wither and die in its shade. And yet, on the spiritual path, we have the audacity to say things like, "If you're afraid, you're not trusting," or, "If you are defending yourself, you've not released the ego-contraction," or, "If you attack an 'other' person, you're really attacking yourself," or, "You can't just use your sexual energy in any way that 'feels' right," or, "Fight or flight mode indicates a lack or deficiency belief." And yet all of these are in fact true.

My opinion, as well as my personal experience, is that all of the ancient esoteric (and monastic) ascetic practices regarding fasting, vigil-keeping (aka meditating through the night with little sleep), celibacy, etc. are not punishment at all, but are natural progressions, and transformed evolutionary levels of our "natural," biological, lower-level counterparts *when a deeper, higher energy and reservoir and identity and source has been tapped* (not before then; for before then would in fact be a masochistic or guilt-ridden road of depletion). In other words, suddenly you don't need what you thought (or were taught) you needed. You don't need as much "sleep" if you meditate regularly, or if the Witness is consciously activated throughout the day and night, or if the frontal lobe is not burnt out on *thinking*. You don't need as much food if you get energy straight from the Source...or from the sun...[129] or if Prana is ingested and assimilated directly from the Universal Energy Field around you. You don't need to release sexual energy if it's not stuck at the 2nd chakra. You don't need to argue or defend or attack if there's no ego-self to be affected. And so on. It's all true. And I can attest, personally, to each one of these transformed "needs."

Both & Beyond

To conclude, I would argue that the interior domain of this reality is as important if not more important than the exterior. Ken would probably say they are equally important, because from a truly nondual perspective, "there is only this," and one is not preferred over the other. I would not disagree. However, to me, the interior is not only infinitely more interesting than the exterior, but also is the domain that we are mostly cut off from even though it is literally right here, and the body doesn't have to go anywhere to explore it. What's more, if something does go on after physical death, it seems obvious that it's the interior, and therefore obvious that it might be important to cultivate that in preparation for that great transition. On the relative side of things, there is most certainly an exact correlate between interior and exterior. For example, Ken says *stages* of development go on theoretically forever (in both directions, all the way up, all the way down, as we've seen).[130] Therefore, on the exterior, our exploration of space and technology and nanobiology and quarks and strings and fractals will go on forever, literally, as long as we are here and there is time. We will never find the edge of the universe. In the same way as you can tune into the interior Ultimate that there is no boundary the other side of which Awareness is not, same is true exteriorly.[131] Similarly, there are lifeforms beneath Magic, and above what Ken calls Supermind. Hence my incorporation of new octaves altogether (above and below). Humans are simply *typically* in *this* octave that progresses like: Magic —> Mythic —> Rational —> Pluralistic (all of which is 1st tier) —> Integral (which is 2nd tier) —> Para-Mind —> Meta-Mind —> Overmind —> Supermind (which are 3rd tier). What happens after that? What happens before that? It's for an altogether different and deeper conversation which necessarily brings into consideration higher intelligences, extraterrestrials, ancient advanced civilizations, and where we go from here.

But both interior and exterior are still arising within...what?...My Awareness (Your Awareness, the Only Awareness); so there is something beyond both holding it all *as* it expands. On the one hand, we could say that when the phenomenal, relative world (of both exterior *and* interior) folds up and comes to a close either at the end of time or at individual death or during meditation practice, You Are That Which Is Left, That Which Remains To Watch It Go. On the other hand, it seems the interior is more lasting, and is at the very least as important as learning how to cook food and brush teeth and put gas (while it lasts) in our vehicles. If the exterior goes when we die, what if what we are left with is whatever we developed of the interior while incarnate in the exterior? What if we had all of our toys and all of our comforts and all of our shallow fillers taken away? Would we be spiritual infants? Would we be interior giants? Would we be prepared to let it all go?

The interior journey and domain runs by similar principles in this regard, but also has its own very unique set of muscles, landscape, texture, capacities, and yes, rules that are very important to learn along the way. While the body lasts, the two do become one. The interior consciousness manifests as and through an exterior body; but to say things like "the soul is trapped inside the body," or "the body is a vehicle" I believe is to sell it short. From the nondual perspective mentioned above, you cannot separate the two. I have a dear yoga student who, after years of "spiritual practice" did not incorporate it into his physical body, and when he began yoga with me said his consciousness was expanding again, to his great surprise. That's because the body had been left out and was now being brought along for the ride! Yoga without a spiritual component is merely exercise or physical therapy. Meditation on the cushion disembodied without the physical is spiritual escapism. The body does in fact get upgrades as consciousness does.

It's as simple as this: *If God is in everything, God is in everything!* So to intentionally or out of fear or denial leave anything out is to spit in the face of God, turn your back on the Source of All, and thus, cut off a piece your very own Ultimate Self. Take it or leave it, but I'm not the only one who says such things. It's part and parcel of the interior life.

The End
(or Back to the Start)

———◆———

As was said at the outset, this book was intentionally written in a casual, conversational tone which seeks to invite the reader not only into the ever-expanding-and-evolving mind of the writer, but also into reading it again, in a sort of "pick-up-anywhere" fashion. It is hoped that you indeed eventually read it all, chapter notes included, but there are many ways to do so, and each different way provides a unique experience and perspective. I also did my best to not make it linearly progressive, which would require you to read it in a particular chronological order in order for it to make sense. At the same time, you won't get the fullest picture until you do get through the whole thing. The world of the writer, and the world of the reader (more specifically, the highly individualized combination of stage, persona, cognitive understanding, experience and proficiency in the Five Basics, and the intersection of that between writer and reader) collide to create a real-time, organic experience—a conversation, between you 'n me. Have it on the coffee table. Have it by the bed. Have it closeby for reference. Again, read it and receive it like a living mosaic (and only one piece in the larger mosaic of my work and offerings—through website, videos, guided meditations, in-person gatherings, and future books; assuming such things are still happening at the time you hold this hard copy in your flesh-hands).

If you don't get something when you start, hang on until the end. And by the time you get to the end, what you already got at the beginning will take root even more deeply as your own implementation of the invitations herein wear their grooves into your being, and you are a more seasoned traveler on the road. The Basics, if I may be so bold, are, though not "un-updatable," pretty solid in their foundational distillation as templates. As I said, a 2nd edition is most certainly in the works, as my own cognitive understanding, experience in my practice, and interaction with students is as we speak growing and maturing. I also gladly, proudly hope to have prepared my shoulders enough to be stood upon safely and sturdily by any who would come along after and see further than I. So get to work!

Chapter Notes

———— ✦ ————

Introduction

1   One study that I no longer have the reference for shows OCD to be in the top ten most debilitating conditions (of not just mental, but of all types) for humans.

2   Really I know it, but I say "believe" because I'm always willing to leave room for other possibilities.

3   One could also say they have continued to do the same to this day, for truly I would not be where I am or who I am without both, equally polar, equally potent; but the difference is what I am about to share in the main text, namely, that because they have been my greatest teachers, I now understand them both far better, and have more of a handle on the shadow, and a deeper perspective on the light. Risking of course this sounding too dualistic (but who cares, anyway?), both were absolutely necessary.

4   I got this information from intrusivethoughts.org, a website that has been a very helpful resource for me in recent times. Surprisingly, when I was younger, I did not "get to know" the disorder from an objective standpoint, and even as I got older and was reading all sorts of books on philosophy, meditation, spiritual practice, etc., I never thought to do my own research on OCD. I believe there are a few reasons for this.

   First, as a kid, I did indeed ask my mom for help with whatever it was going on in my head, but when she suggested a psychologist, I said No. Being in the South in the early 90s, however, there was no such awareness of alternative treatment, meditation, yoga, "plant medicine," shamans, or—sheesh!—monasteries! Some cultures, who have this kind of thing as a normal part of their collective understanding, would've been keen to the experiences I was having and celebrated that another spiritual "seer" or teacher had been born, and the parents would've taken that child to the shaman, the sage, the master so that they could be trained in the ways appropriate to what was happening and what they were being called to. Now, by no fault of her own, my mother didn't know any better. She did take me to our pastor, but bless his heart too (for he was indeed an important early mentor) he couldn't handle my questions either, and was no sage, just a gentle-hearted, soft-spoken, Bible-minded man not prepared for the likes of me—none of 'em were, and I don't blame them. I had to go my own way anyway. In any case, I'm the one who asked for help, but the help provided was not what I really needed. Neither did I want medication, but that's just what you did for people exhibiting my symptoms. I believe there was a knowing deep down that none of the labels fit—mental disorder, saved and now going to heaven, or called to be a Southern Baptist preacher. So I didn't bother "getting to know" my "disease," while at the same time didn't know how else to categorize it, so I abhorred and loathed the identity slapped onto me from the outside—*I have OCD and I take however-many milligrams of Luvox, or* (later) *Paxil, and that's that* was the interior script I was fed and had no choice but to believe.

Secondly, as the main text is now addressing, I had countless psychologists and psychiatrists and talk therapists and behavior therapists and fundamentalist Christian mentors and teachers and people who tried their darndest to help me. But none of that, and I mean *none* of that, did *any* good. Some of it, though now understood as perfectly part of my journey, was actually harmful. Nothing worked until I discovered the experiential rather than dogmatic systems of yoga, meditation, Eastern healing arts, and truly psychoactive practices (not penitential punishments), which did span the spectrum all the way from contemplative and monastic Christian to yogic to Integral to New Age to Buddhist to Hindu (specifically Advaita Vedanta) approaches. And not only did these practices allow me to discontinue my medication for good, but also simply vanquished many of my most cumbersome symptoms—just poof, gone! And as my identity in general began to shift beyond the personality or relative self altogether, I knew directly now that no label or definition or contraction or any *thing* imposed by conditioning whatsoever was truly, Ultimately, who I am.

With this, I gladly tossed the OCD diagnosis out the window. Rather than *I have OCD*, the new script (both to myself as well as to others) was *I was diagnosed with OCD when I was a kid*. In the past. Long gone. Bye-bye. So again, no need to "study" OCD, because I didn't actually <u>have</u> it! Plus I was still wrestling with my opinion that I was mistreated, misdiagnosed, mishandled when it all first started. So I moved into a phase of slight denial, resentment, and pride (and understandably so) because everybody tried to, but nobody could, help me. *I helped myself goddam it! and I don't need drugs and don't need diagnoses and don't need docs!*

I've come around to a sort of full circle now, and occasionally have bouts with some old familiar friends, or fiends, from the deeply embedded program. But I know how to handle it now; and I have a wife who has been more supportive, understanding, and helpful—skillfully walking the fine line between allowing my idiosyncrasies but not perpetuating the problem—than anyone I've ever been in any kind of partnership with, personal or professional. I do not and will not ever need medication again. I just do my practice, that's what I'm trying to say, and that's why what I teach means so much to me. The work presented in this book is my lifeblood, is what healed me, is what makes me whole, is what saved my life. Literally.

Still, however, to this day, the conglomeration of what it is, what it was, what I am, what I have, who I am, and what happened on that fateful night is a great mystery. A mystery that I don't necessarily want to solve or figure out, because I know that the perfect unfolding creates the tension necessary for transformation—I wouldn't be writing this book for you without it, for one.

But back to the reason I started this note: I've never had much of an interest, for these various reasons, to really study OCD as a "thing": on the one hand, I've always known that, for me at least, it's more than a simple clinical diagnosis based on a few indicators in the DSM-IV (the operative manual at the time; it's now the DSM-V); and even if it were merely that, I've never wanted it to be a crutch—there's no excuse, and the mind is the mind is the mind is the mind, and the power of God, the power of this work, is stronger than any thought pattern, neurotic, psychotic, or not. However, it has been helpful and interesting and insightful to, at this point in my journey, have the resource of some videos and articles and documentaries simply to understand the program a little better, and intrusivethoughts.org has been great for just that very purpose. Again, I plan to write a much more thorough treatise and reflection specifically on OCD (and how this work relates with mental illness and poorly integrated spiritual experience) one day. But suffice it to say on the one hand, it would be very difficult to diagnose me now based on the current DSM criteria, and on the other hand, when I'm in a triggered state, sure I have OCD; but who cares?! Doesn't everyone have a little bit of all of it? And it ain't like it used to be, I ain't who I used to be, and that's all that matters. All of this and more is why I do not subscribe to "once an addict always an addict" or "once diagnosed always diagnosed." Okay, back to the main text.

5   Again, this kind of prayer is a form of meditation, to be sure, and indeed at the time was coming from a very Magic/Mythic mindset and understanding of God and "Who" I was talking to, but as with everything else, it was necessary, and did not fall on deaf ears. The purpose of this section is to show how meditation, in all of its facets and functions (prayer, contemplation, interior inquiry, connection with and devotion and surrender to the Divine by whatever name) has followed me "all the days of my life" (reference to Psalm 23:6) and has been my constant companion in the darkest of days; has shaped me and made me soft, and strong, in the hands of One greater than I. [Remove all religious, dogmatic interpretation, please, and insert direct relationship and experiential communion.]

6   That's a term I'd come up with later, and I have since taken my own path far beyond his instruction; but his practical introduction, without the spiritual bells and whistles, was a superb way to start.

7   Reference to Philippians 1:6

8   In fact, one of my students recently asked me if I regret some of the things I said when I was a teenage fundamentalist preacher (basically coming from the Magic/Mythic stage). I said definitely not, because I now understand that it was a stage among stages (and from Integral and above it is seen that every stage previous has a perfect part to play, even now. So I was simply preaching from and to the Magic/Mythic world, and just so happened to not stay there. I also was prone to share vulnerably (as I still do) about my personal journey and struggles, say things that stretched and challenged my listeners, and intimately talk about my personal relationship with God, all of which was a little uncomfortable for some of the people at those levels. Inherent in the lower stages is a judgmental and fearful attitude toward others not in the club; but this never felt right to me, so even when I preached, as a teenager, I never came from that place, and never threatened hell on anybody. That, perhaps, would've caused some regret. I myself was working out interiorly the ways that certain pieces of the puzzle didn't seem to fit right, so I did not impose what I already saw as the weakness (before I even knew what stages were), or burden anyone with what I was wrestling with. I kept that pretty close to my chest. While my hope is to assist in the turning of the conveyor belt of consciousness, and I wish that folks didn't linger too long or get stuck and slip into a pathological version or a lower stage, the Magic and Mythic stages are beautiful in their own ways and I still draw on their true essence, holding them and all others in my "transcending and including" Integral embrace (as Ken would say).

9   I do indeed have a lot to say about the mindless transference of rockstar worship onto a "guru" from the Magic level, or from a

Magic subpersonality, and our world of spiritual celebrity in general, which Jesus himself dealt with and did not appreciate, and which I do speak on in the moment if I feel it happening, but I will save that for another time. Here, I am simply referring to my own process with being on the receiving end of the public's predictable pattern of projection and my own intention of authenticity.

10 Galatians 5:22-23

11 translation by Stephen Mitchell; brackets mine

12 In my opinion and experience, if you put in the work, it's inevitable. But you have to let go of the timeline, and it may or may not happen in this lifetime. But the work has been logged and you are further along with every little bit. In Zen, Enlightenment is called a "happy accident"; in Psalms 130:6, it is said, "My soul waits for the Lord more than watchmen wait for the morning"; in Matthew (25:1), Jesus tells of brides keeping their candles trimmed and burning as they wait on their groom to arrive; A Course In Miracles says that the first step and the last step are both taken by God; and St. Paul says, "...he who began a good work in you will bring it to completion..." (Philippians 1:6). All of these references imply doing your work and then trusting a greater Wisdom to finish the job. So while it's not really "luck," it is most certainly now out of your hands; but anyone who has ever dared to take such a leap has never been disappointed.

13 All that I am saying will be received and understood in a much fuller way if the reader understands Ken Wilber's AQAL framework, or at least his category of Stages, though this is not necessarily a requirement. I have chosen not to give an entire section on Stages in this book because for a sufficient enough treatment, it would take up too much space and would dilute the concentration of the Five Basics. Therefore the omission is quite the contrary of absent. I am not me without Ken; and I am taking his work to the next level (pun intended/not intended). For an introduction, at the time of this publication, I have a four-part video series on my website, under the Videos tab, basically titled

Stages 1, Stages 2, Stages 3, Stages 4. If you would like further introduction to Ken's work, read his Integral Spirituality and/or listen to his audio-interview with Tami Simon called The 1-2-3 of God (a Sounds True production).

Meditation Practice

14 Gross here does not mean yucky, though not an inaccurate play on words. It's a technical term referring to the physical, waking realm in which mindless, analytical thinking in general takes place. The self operative there is usually the one who got you into trouble in the first place, which is why any attempts by that one to fix the problem will inevitably and universally fail, and why taking off the mask is of utmost importance to make progress on the interior journey and have a successful meditation practice. As grace would have it, meditation itself, if done properly, takes off the mask for you (so you don't have to do it yourself!). The mask metaphor really cannot be overdone, and I return to it again and again.

15 There is also a lot of research being done in more mainstream science circles (for any who care to come from that perspective) confirming what the interior traditions have always known, practiced, and taught—from biology to neurobiology to psychology and others—which is why meditation is becoming so popular these days... However, my approach still takes it further, beyond what the mainstream is usually willing to engage or admit, and while I present a few facts here and there, I don't need objective science to prove what I have found experientially. Nonetheless, it is an important contribution to the conversation, so, if you'd like to dive into that field to supplement what we're doing here, there are mounds of information about the benefits of meditation from a secular "hard science" perspective.

16 There's no set rule about "regular basis," but if you're really going for it, 20 minutes every day is minimum; 20 minutes twice a day is ideal; and up and up from there at your discretion based on your

lifestyle and schedule and intensity of desire for progress on the path. You can't overshoot this one; the more the better, really. But it is absolutely crucial to check in regularly with a teacher who understands the process, especially if your frequency is higher than once a day. What I'm saying is, shit's gonna come up. That's part of it and to be expected. So be ready for a wild and beautiful ride.

17   This is, of course, only if you're doing everything outlined in this book. If you're not, you might just be sick, in which case, go to the doctor!

18   I had one particularly memorable incident when I was just beginning this journey and was meditating quite a bit in which as I "came out" of a particular 20 minute sit, instantly a sharp pain in my stomach emerged that cycled through for the next 24 hours. With it was dizziness, cold sweats, black outs, dry heaves, and what felt like food poisoning. Upon contacting the restaurant where I had eaten dinner (a simple salad with no meat, by the way) and finding out no one else had reported being sick, and remembering that my then mentor had warned me (with the same warning I am giving you now), I realized it was directly connected to the practice, to the work, and to the fact that it happened while visiting a prospective grad school in Chicago with my mom (all of which was right on target with an emotional, umbilical, letting-go, and leaving-the-nest nexus-knot).

19   The traditions vary widely on the Ultimates, but agree on the fact that they are "always already" there, and therefore technically speaking are not states, because states by definition come and go. Regardless, however, there is a clear line between "knowing" they are, and conscious mindful awareness in their always-alreadiness.

20   The interior vs. exterior distinction is obviously quite important for the purposes of this book, and besides touching on it in regards to interior vs. exterior traditions (i.e., esoteric vs. exoteric, etc.) I briefly go into it again in the Interior Domain chapter. But, as I've said, for a fuller understanding of what Ken calls the 4 Quadrants

(interior and exterior of individual and collective), read any of his later books, most recommendedly Integral Spirituality.

21   I want to come right out and say that the entire Hindu, Vedic, and Yogic compendium is immeasurably rich and complex with detail and description, the meaning and interpretation of which cannot be divorced from its own original culture, and any Western attempt at "spiritual reductionism" will without a doubt be a disgrace to the first seers who wrote it all down. This very fact is in and of itself an indication of how poised these masters were at observing and recording the interior workings of the human experience. So I do not and will not pretend that the examples from which I draw parallels are "exactly" the same as what they were saying. We are forever indebted to their contribution, and can only wish to see a fraction. But we must start somewhere, and try to stand on their shoulders if we dare. We also like to mix-and-match to meet our needs, and this does not always serve us in the long run. That's why they call us, in the States, the melting pot, right? I am admitting now that in the current paragraph of the main text I am drawing loose parallels and merging a few systems together simply to make a point. The same is true for other ancient systems like Tibetan Buddhism and Kabbalah—indelibly accurate, specific, and culturally contained.

In addition, at the time of this publication, scientists have begun to discover "brain cells" in the heart and the gut, indicating the possibility that the brain that is housed in the skull is not the only brain in the body! Therefore, when I say that the mental body can be measured with EEG machines, that's only part of the picture as we're now coming to understand.

And one more technicality: The mental body of the energy field is the exterior component in the energetic realm. The mental body of the brain (and now possibly heart and gut) is the exterior component in the physical realm. Perhaps these details point to the endless sophistication of the maps mentioned two paragraphs up. I, again, have chosen a more casual and approachable tone here, with technicalities pointed out sporadically. Mostly I am hoping to give you some pointers and tools for you to extrapolate on your own. Were I to break each item down with my academic prowess, like Ken does, well, you see how long his books are, and you'd probably never pick it up. Just know that I know that I'm leaving some stuff out...

22   I make a distinction between attention and Awareness, which is covered further in the Ultimates chapter. Though with a low-ercase "a," awareness could also be synonymous with what I call attention, for the sake of clarification, I use attention in that relative case, and Awareness with a capital "A" for the Ultimate. Relatively, attention can come and go; or attention can be on this thing and not on that other thing; or attention can be more or less focused or relaxed; or attention can be stronger or weaker; or attention can be intentionally moved around. Awareness, however, is an Ultimate "always-already," and is always-already as-it-is, the same, constant. You can do nothing to make Awareness happen, not happen, increase, or decrease. You can, however, paradoxically turn your attention toward It, which brings It into "conscious awareness," eventually shifting identity from the individual self to That-Which-Is-Aware-of-It. And, paradoxically, the more evolved the individual self is, the richer the experience of Awareness is. But again, for more on Awareness, and the distinction between relatives and Ultimates, see The Ultimates chapter. For our purposes now, we are talking about attention, or mindfulness, which is a practiced and trainable skill, and a movable scope, if you will, to all times and dimensions and things.

23   I also use the word "see" to mean awareness or observation of any thing in any dimension that you (as relative you or Ultimate You) are aware of. So "see" can be interchangeable with "experience," "witness," "observe," "hear," "feel," etc. For instance, you can see a sound by simply noticing it. You can see a sensation by feeling it. You can see a thought by witnessing it.

24   This is from our current commonly accepted paradigm, of course,

which only from the fringes takes into account the possibility of the heart and the gut being brains with their own patterns and waves as well, and a newly discovered, not-yet-fully-understood Gamma wave that has been measured among some Buddhist monks.

25   Some long-time meditators claim to maintain conscious aware-ness throughout all states of sleeping; i.e., lucid dreaming and the Nothingness or Void of deep dreamless sleep. This is not a re-quirement nor a gold-star achievement; it's just a possibility, and there are lots of practices that you can learn to "achieve" this as well if interested; I'm just not an expert there. Those who I've heard report it first-hand say it happened naturally, simply as a progression of meditation, and that it wasn't anything they tried to attain. What I'm pointing to is the possibility of consciously maintaining attentive awareness in all of those same states of consciousness on the meditation cushion. Therefore, it bears clarifying that the difference between meditating and sleeping is not brain waves nor bed vs cushion nor lying vs sitting, but con-scious awareness (or mindfulness) itself.

26   It seems silly to have to say, but if practicing mindfulness while driving, please maintain the proper amount of focus necessary to stay on the road and stay safe.

27   We could even say that relaxed, attentive awareness of mindless-ness, or of idle/autopilot thoughts is a good place to start; and while on the one hand, we are hoping to retrain the neural path-ways into mindful, peaceful thoughts, on the other hand, from a Witnessing or Nondual perspective (which we hit on in the Ultimates chapter), these are no longer shunned if and when they do occur.

28   A term popularly used for the athletic flow state is "the zone." Athletes of all levels and variety (stellar, novice, intermediate, "just for fun," children as well as adults) will, on occasion, accidentally slip into an above-average, elite space in which they themselves say things like, "I felt unstoppable," and their opponents reflect

the same—"I couldn't stop him." Or, "I just felt like I couldn't miss!" My friend and colleague Scott Ford is a tennis pro who has harnessed this ever-elusive holy grail of sports in his book Integral Consciousness and Sport: Unifying Body, Mind, and Spirit Through Flow, and in his technique that he calls "The Parallel Mode Process." Rather than the zone being merely happenstance, and rather than simply coaching athletes to "be better" at their sport, he teaches a way to focus (in particular the eyes and the mind) that induces this expanded state across many different sports. I was coached by Scott with this technique in both tennis and basketball, and experienced instant and profound acceleration of my already pretty solid abilities in each (not to mention spiritual insights and meditative implications). According to him, he's also worked with hockey and baseball players with the same results. I've seen him take brand new tennis beginners who were astonished themselves at how quickly they picked up not only the game but the flow state as well. Needless to say, and this obviously approaches the edge of our scope in this book, there is a considerable need for Scott's contribution in the very low-stage-of-consciousness, ego-based world of competitive sports. Check out his work if this resonates with you.

29 Eventually the technique is no-technique (no training wheels needed, so to speak), when simply engaging the interior muscle, and/or intending the direction, is enough.

30 Some would say there is plenty of good stuff in the OBE realm, and I'd say that's true as well; I'm not belittling any area anyone would like to consciously cultivate. I spent considerable time training myself for astral travel, and even went to a week-long retreat for that very purpose, and only had one very brief (and forgettable) experience. I have instances during the night sometimes when I feel I'm speeding down a tunnel, or hovering weightlessly over my bed, so I'm sure I've gone on some adventures and just don't remember. But still, my work, my practice, my world is in the Causal and beyond. Stay tuned. I'm getting to that in the main text.

31   There is a brilliant movie currently on Netflix called The Discovery that portrays some of the things we're talking about. The current assumption about dreams is that the dreamer is the only one aware of their dream (because it's the individual interior), while the only thing people on the exterior can know is the brain waves (if the person is hooked up to machines), which in and of themselves mean nothing. This movie challenges such a notion, and whether it's mere sci-fi or future possibility, time will tell.

32   Which, by the way, speaking of transition points, it is totally possible to train your meditation "muscle" so that not only do you maintain consciousness throughout all the states, but that you remain aware during the crossover, or the threshold between states as the brain waves shift gears. So, just as in the Ultimates chapter I talk about infinite increments in a relative spectrum in which you have to draw the line somewhere, and a tipping point when the dial has been turned to the next noticeable frequency, same with brain waves. As Beta starts to slow down and become Alpha, it doesn't just switch over all at once, but there is indeed a moment when it's no longer Beta anymore. In the same way, as Alpha starts to become Theta, it gets closer and closer and closer until in a flash Alpha is Theta; as well as from Theta to Delta and so on. There is a lot of research being done, particularly by The Monroe Institute, regarding exactly what combination of brain waves are required (on the exterior) to induce a desired experience (on the interior). The sleep cycle goes in the same order as the meditation cycle, but during meditation, you can "on purpose" maintain a particular state for a longer, sustained period of time.

    The point is to say that if you train your ability strong enough, you will not flash out as waking becomes hypnagogic becomes *Theta* becomes *Delta*. Awareness is the same throughout anyway, right? What's different is the specific body or relative sense of self that experiences each state. If you can anchor into Pure, Ultimate Awareness during the transitions into the new bodies and the new selves, then that's the magic; rather than a blackout, blank space, and then suddenly back online. Make sense? This again is possible sleeping as well as meditating, but to date I have not had any lucid sleeping experiences (to my memory), so I am speaking mostly about meditation. (As one more quick aside, don't ask me about R.E.M. or out-of-body experiences or astral traveling; I simply don't have much knowledge or direct experience with either, though I did go through a period in which I was very interested in OBE's, and the work of Robert Monroe. Explore that at your leisure on your own. I will say that my first meditation teacher taught us a trick to induce relaxation, which was to move the eyes quickly back and forth, left and right, to mimic R.E.M. and drop in more quickly to a meditative state. For me, it was more frustrating than effective, but sure enough, it works.)

33   There is a caution to not get caught up too much in what's being experienced, lest the ego attach to the content and abort the subconscious unloading process that needs to happen in releasing samskara.

34   More on the relative self and Ultimate Self in the Who Am I? chapter.

35   There is so much more to say about this, but suffice it to say, for now, that it may have something to do with the fractalized, holographic, simulated nature of our reality. I personally don't believe we're supposed to figure it out in this realm. We're supposed to search for the answer and never find it the way we want—but if the search is the right one, we find an Answer that vanquishes all questions. We have new and amazing insights, breakthroughs, and revelations (both scientific and spiritual) along the way, but again, they thought the atom was the most basic particle; then they split the atom. They thought the universe was fixed; then they realized it's actually pulling apart at breakneck speeds into oblivion. Same with interior consciousness—into a black hole, out through a white, expand, contract, liberate, integrate, endlessly forever. But there has always and already been a route

THE UNNAMED KALIANA WAY

to freedom, beyond time and space (interior and exterior), and that's the gateway of the Ultimates.

36   Some say that deep dreamless sleep every night is not to rest the body, but is to rest the soul. I have a theory that this is why our individual finite consciousness unplugs entirely from "this world," and could be potentially going "home," wherever home is, to rejuvenate. This is a wild one, but still, sleep is a most strange phenomenon with a lot of unanswered mystery surrounding it.

37   Translation by Stephen Mitchell (my brackets)

38   In fact, for me, sometimes it actually feels like the eyes are open. I won't draw quick conclusions that this is the "third eye" or something super spiritual like that (though it could be); but it is one among the many strange phenomena that can occur.

39   Drunvalo Melchizedek's The Ancient Secret of the Flower of Life is a great place to start.

40   As a quick aside, imagination does not mean "not real"; it simply means the part of your consciousness where images reside and are formed. Images are projected out to the exterior and reflected back as "objects," but the image (and the object) still remains interior. Cutting edge optical sciences are confirming this, and the work of Jacob Liberman is pioneering in this field. So much more to say, but I'll save it...

41   This is a very interesting turn of phrase, and a strong indicator that Buechner has some experience into these states meditatively. For someone who has not looked and seen, they might very well say something like this, i.e., "I am a body." But of course, even our grammar and way of speaking about "ourselves" proves immediately that this is not true. We speak of the body as "mine" ("My head hurts," "My muscles are sore," "My heart skipped a beat."), and Buechner would be speaking from a very immature and underdeveloped sense of spiritual sight if he literally meant, in a pre-rational sort of fused way that he is his body. A very potent practice of self-inquiry technique is to name any thing in your awareness and say, "I can observe _____, therefore I am not

_____," "I am witnessing _____, therefore I am not _____," "I see/hear/feel/experience _____, therefore I am not _____," etc. Buechner is clearly speaking from a beyond-rational perspective, or perhaps we could say a Nondual (which we cover in more detail in the Ultimates chapter...) experience of Oneness.

42 From Wikipedia, "Tohu wa-bohu...is a Biblical Hebrew phrase found in the Genesis creation narrative...that describes the condition of the earth...immediately before the creation of light..."

43 Excerpt from The Alphabet of Grace, published by Harper San Francisco, 1970.

The Ultimates

44 a. Ken Wilber is one who has only these two Ultimates (which he calls Absolutes), and sometimes uses their Sanskrit words from the Upanishads, turiya and turiyatita. I do not know if Ken personally would delineate more than two but has chosen for ease of teaching and communicating to keep it simple, but this is one area in which I am taking his work further. I know he doesn't mind...

b. I will say at the outset of this chapter that language gets tricky when talking about the Ultimates because of the dualistic nature of words and sentence structure. So where necessary (and as best I can) I use capital and lowercase letters intentionally to designate Ultimate vs. relative, respectively; and I use quotation marks to indicate a sort of "this-but-not-exactly-this" paradoxical understanding. That doesn't mean that's what I'm doing every time I use quotes or capitals, and it's sort of a shame that we don't have more linguistic tools for such transcendent truth (alas, a culture's written language says a lot about its collective understanding and preoccupations); but we'll get through it together. Sometimes the word "ultimate" itself speaks for itself and I don't need to capitalize it. Or to capitalize "That-Which-Is" makes it "a thing" that I am making more important than other things by capitalizing it and therefore is made not Ultimate by trying to make it so. Technically, anything said about the Ultimate is already not the Ultimate and contradictorily cancels itself out.

Some writers who understand this make an entire style out of not capitalizing anything, or capitalizing too much, or using quotes too often. Or some lose their readers in an overbearing need to clarify every little possible contradiction (but then every clarification does the same thing and needs clarification if they're doing it correctly). It's a delicate balance—for even those, in their attempt to portray the Absolute, can become obsessed with the very task and the obsessive contraction itself misses the point entirely. It's a fun challenge for a writer concerned with these realities, and there is a calling for a new way of expressing the inexpressible poetically and artistically (my contribution to this can be found in my *Nowhere to Now-Here* series, and other books I plan to write later down the road).

45 From here forward, Ultimate state will refer to one of these "always-alreadies," and may be interchangeable with "always-already" as a noun, or "always, already" as an adjective. Though "state" may be used, they are not states as such, for they do not "come and go" as do relative states, which include waking, dreaming, deep sleep, and any sub-states within those primary states (such as a state of anger, a state of anxiety, a state of frustration, a state of happiness, a state of peace, etc.) Relative states require, and are correlated with, a change in brain wave pattern and other exterior changes in body, nervous system, and all the exterior parallels of layers aka body in general (covered in the kosha section), and somewhat of an interior movement to "get there," whether that movement is falling asleep or employing a meditation technique or becoming agitated or becoming excited. Though Ultimate states may also be accompanied by a change in brain wave pattern and body, the only requirement to "get there" is to remove all obstacles to seeing it; and across the board, when the inquiry is made, "Was there a time or place when or where this was not the case," the answer is an emphatically obvious, "No." The only change was that the finite self turned its attention toward That Which Always Already Is, and there only seemed to be a time when it was not. This paradox is covered further in the Who Am I section.

46 Sama means "together" and is where we get our word "same," and dhi or dha means something like "to place" (to place together, therefore, is, again, not so different from the etymology of religion and Yoga). So Samadhi is an Ultimate state of Union or Oneness of self (immanent), God (transcendent), and all things (manifest). Something like this.

47 In my opinion, we do this too often. We are blessed in the West to have such a melting pot of rich spiritual traditions at our disposal. But the shadow side of such a melting pot is sometimes the specifics get blurred together and the potency diluted because the vine has been uprooted from its original soil. So, part of my intention, in a similar way as Ken Wilber has done, is to make sense of all the traditions for our own integrated, contemporary, specifically American, society. On that note, it's even difficult to even say what "American food" is, or what spiritual traditions are uniquely American. But that's what makes us unique (the new kids on the block that have a lot to offer as well as a lot to learn). In ancient cultures like China, Japan, and India, the spirituality is seamlessly woven into the tapestry of the larger culture, and children are immersed in it from birth (which in and of itself, of course, comes with its own limitations). So, utilizing all of my studies, training, mentors' guidance, and personal experience and perspective, I seek to make sense of it all for us, for you, today, in context as well as beyond conditioning.

48 There is a paradox here as well. The always-alreadyness does not change, and the basic flavor of the specific Ultimate does not change (for example, Ultimate Presence is still different from Ultimate Awareness is still different from Ultimate Present Moment), but as the finite self grows and matures and evolves and heals, the way in which the non-experienceable is experienced is slightly (or profoundly) different. Eventually, as third-tier (Ken Wilber's term) dawns, the finite self becomes so expanded that it is tough to tell the difference between itself and the Ultimate. But that's another story as well. See Ken's The Religion of Tomorrow for a wonderful synopsis of third-tier states and stages.

49 Except when the relative is seen from the Nondual perspective as infused with, and none-other-than, the Ultimate. Getting the gist?

50 Which means, God and enlightenment as things to grasp are not Ultimate God and Enlightenment.

51 If you've never thought about it, you may think that eternity and infinity are interchangeable as words and therefore as concepts. But technically, and this is important, eternity refers to time, and infinity refers to space. When I was a kid, and the grown-ups were talking about eternity in heaven, my adolescent, Magic-level cognition interpreted it to mean endless time in a confined place. It actually sounded more like hell, but I couldn't figure out how to get around it, and thus smiled and nodded like a good little boy and pretended like I was so very excited to be there "one day" when I die. Weird! Unfortunately, many (or most) adults are still stuck in this low stage of interpretation when it comes to spiritual or religious understanding. So, relative eternity is endless time; relative infinity is endless space. Ultimate Eternity is Present Moment beyond time; Ultimate Infinity is Presence, Here beyond spatiality.

52 Realistically, we could have only Four Basics, where Ultimate vs relative Who Am I? is included in this chapter, and the relative self is included in the Responsibility chapter. But Ramana Maharshi says that the only tool you need for your knapsack to realize enlightenment or your true self is the inquiry Who Am I? Therefore I felt it fitting to give it its own chapter. I do not put any of the Five Basics above the others in weight or degree of importance, and as we've already seen, they each interrelate with all of the others.

53 To extrapolate a bit further on this... Within the relative plane, on a given polarized relative spectrum, as we just saw, the increments proceed in infinite degrees forever in both directions (even if outside of our standard human bandwidth of perception, theoretically, or even detected by sophisticated instruments, it is seen that it goes on forever). So, to take our "half-the-distance-to-the-wall"

example, let's go the other direction. If my teacher doubled her distance away from the wall, and then doubled it again, and again, and again...besides now being far enough away that we could've left unnoticed and skipped school the rest of the day...would she ever reach the Ultimate? No! Would she ever reach the end of the "distance away from the wall" spectrum? No! Is there a wall or boundary the other side of which she could not continue beyond with ever increasing distances away from the original? No. Out and out and out, in and in and in. All still relative. But the spectrum itself does have a beginning and end in time and space. What's more, remember, if it has a beginning in time, it has a beginning in space. If it has a beginning in space, it has a beginning in time. Also remember, the phenomenal world (which is by definition a relative, or a happening, or a thing) does not just include the visual, physical, exterior world that we typically preference as "real." Even the highest vibrations of light, beyond what the human eye can see, or the lowest vibrations of sound, below what the human ear can hear, or the furthest reaches of outer space or the deepest reaches of inner space, including thoughts and states of consciousness, however profound or dense—all still relative. We are being shown by our cutting edge sciences that time is as malleable as space, and that "otherworldly beings" can manipulate both in their interdimensional travel; i.e., wormholes, portals, folding the continuum on itself. All. Still. Relative. The Ultimate is the Ultimate is the Ultimate, no matter who or what you are; but, as we see in other sections, the experience of the Ultimate paradoxically is determined by your unique vantage point and viewpoint and stage of consciousness, which includes technological as well as psycho-spiritual evolution or devolution, and the particular bodyform inhabited. So, for example, plants have the same Ultimate, but the plant's experience (and yes, plants have experiences, are also in the sentient family) of the Ultimate is unique to its form; rocks have the same Ultimate, but the rock's experience (and yes, rocks have experiences too, and though some may argue with me, are also in the sentient family) of the Ultimate is unique to its form; deer have the same Ultimate, but the deer's experience of the Ultimate is unique to its form; smartphones have the same Ultimate, but the smartphone's experience (ok, getting a little far out now..? Don't take my word for it, though; think about it. Everything has sentience, or prehension, or perception of some vibration. What about A.I.?) of the Ultimate is unique to its form; humans have the same Ultimate, but humans' (and beings beyond human) experience of the Ultimate is unique to their form. Humans may be unique, or most highly evolved neurologically (at least in potential; in actual is another question), than other species "native" to our planet, in that they are the first, or only, ones to have self-reflexive, or self-aware capabilities; meaning humans can be aware of being aware, or can sit around and contemplate this Ultimate. Research (and a lot of assumptions) indicate that animals and plants and artificial intelligence cannot. That does not make them less sentient or less held by the same Ultimate, or even less experiencing or deserving of the same Ultimate. The experience is just different, more or less complex if you will. Take Rainer Maria Rilke's words in this excerpt from "The Eighth Duino Elegy" as something in this regard to contemplate:

Animals see the unobstructed
world with their whole eyes.
But our eyes, turned back upon
themselves, encircle and
seek to snare the world,
setting traps for freedom.
The faces of the beasts
show what truly IS to us:
we who up-end the infant and
force its sight to fix upon
things and shapes, not the

freedom that they occupy,
that openness which lies so deep
within the faces of the animals,
free from death!
We alone face death.
The beast, death behind and
God before, moves free through
eternity like a river running.
Never for one day do we
turn from forms to face
that place of endless purity
blooming flowers forever know.
Always a world for us, never
the nowhere minus the no:
that innocent, unguarded
space which we could breathe,
know endlessly, and never require.
A child, at times, may lose
himself within the stillness
of it, until rudely ripped away.
Or one dies and IS the place.
As death draws near,
one sees death no more, rather
looks beyond it with, perhaps,
the broader vision of the beasts.
...
We are, above all, eternal spectators
looking upon, never from,
the place itself. We are the
essence of it. We construct it.
It falls apart. We reconstruct it
and fall apart ourselves.
...
-translated by Robert Hunter, found on hunterarchive.com

This does not mean animals and babies are more evolved, but that they have less snags against which to see the Ultimate; they just ARE it on a certain level, the same way as every phenomenon IS it on that same certain level. And while there is less obstruction to SEE it, there is perhaps less depth and expanse OF it. This is what we are referring to when we say that the Ultimate is unchanging except in the relative experience of the one experiencing It. Ken's *pre/trans fallacy* would be appropriate to the conversation here. It's a matter of *relative* evolution and identity (which again, we get to in the Who Am I? chapter). In any case, and to return to our point, *if it has a beginning and an end in time and space, it is relative*. The Ultimate is something else entirely. Sort of.

54 translation by Daniel Ladinsky

55 Matthew 6:33, RSV; brackets and italics mine

56 I Corinthians 15:55, RSV; brackets mine

57 Jesus in Matthew 7:16

58 We won't even get into the fact that "a year" itself is relative and is specific to our planet and our solar system alone.

59 But is arising as always where it's always arisen: in your Awareness, Here, Now. That's another story that we'll get to shortly.

60 I had a student say that he could not parse out the difference between "I," "here," and "now." My answer was something along the lines of relative vs ultimate versions of each one (to coincide with my perspective that there are many flavors of the Ultimate, and that each one has a relative correlate as well). So, I has a relative and Ultimate sense of "self" and "identity"; Here has a relative and Ultimate sense of presence and location or non-local positioning regarding space; "Now" has a relative and Ultimate sense of present moment, time, or timelessness. Ram Dass, bless his soul, found some kind of primordial Trinity of perception in his injunction Be Here Now.

61 All of which are relative, and therefore are of relative importance; which means they are important, yes, but when priorities are rearranged, they can be more easily enjoyed or let go of as such.

62 This also means interiorly. It doesn't necessarily mean with physical measuring instruments like rulers and scales; those are included, but also, the measurement of intensity of a sensation, the measurement of the relative beginning and ending of a thought, the length of suffering, the weight of an emotion.

63 "You" here is contextual as well, because as "you" recognize the Ultimates more and more, the realization is obvious that you are them, they are you, and that any relative you is, well, only a relative you. Of course you are everything and all things at once, but your center of gravity/identity can presume itself to be a relative, finite you and can turn itself away from the sun, so to speak, thus casting a shadow, or be identified on the ground side of the clouds. But if you are the sun, you can never turn away from yourself; and if you are on the sun side of the clouds, you see that the sun never stops shining.

64 Because, technically, you are always in touch with them; just more or less consciously.

65 In traditional Zen culture, the teacher will give the student one koan at a time, and will not give the next one until the student has successfully accessed the "state" being pointed to. Each one gets progressively more difficult, which means some koans are wrestled with for months and years before a new one is given. I believe there is benefit to this way, and I also believe there is benefit to the way I have laid it out. On the one hand, my "one per day" prescription could be seen as a reflection of impatiently jumping from one thing to the next, but on the other, as I am conscious of upgrading ancient traditions while preserving their qualitative depth, I believe the frustration of "not getting it" could in fact trigger our cultural impatience and the student may give up, and if they simply move on to the next one, the next one may be the one that does the trick. Note: my list is not in any order of difficulty.

66 "[God] spoke one word, and speaks always in eternal silence, and in silence has it been heard by the soul." (St. John of the Cross, my translation from the original Spanish.)

67 Psalm 139:7-10 (my paraphrase): Where could I possibly go away from Your Spirit? Where could I run from Your Presence? If I ascend to heaven, You are there! If I descend to the underworld, You are there! If I fly to the future horizon, or live in the depths of the sea, even there Your hand shall lead me, guide me, and hold me safe.

68 reference to Isaiah 58:11

69 St. Teresa of Avila is known to have said that she simply sits like a limp dishrag until God calls her to move, because moving of her own accord or strength would be weakness to God (this is akin to the repeated theme throughout St. Paul's letters regarding God's strength in his weakness).

70 These writers among others in the Absurdity of Existence genre/ philosophical approach of literature.

71 Jason Upton, "No Sacrifice": "Your thoughts are higher than mine/Your words are deeper than mine," reference to Isaiah 55:8-9 (RSV): "For my thoughts are not your thoughts, neither are your ways my ways, says the LORD. For as the heavens are higher than the earth, so are my ways higher than your ways and my thoughts than your thoughts."

72 St. Thomas Aquinas, re: why he had stopped writing: "I cannot, for everything I have written seems to me like straw."

73 When nothing means anything, anything means everything.

Taking Responsibility

74 When Freud's work was being translated from German to English, every time he wrote "I" (in German Ich), his translator for whatever reason decided to use the Latin "ego" instead of the English "I," and thus, the commonly accepted English neologism "ego," with all of its spiritual meaning, was born. So any time you hear about Freud's theory of the ego, he himself was simply saying "the I." See how that changes some things? See how important language is? Other translation anomalies happened around the id and Superego as well, but we won't go into those now.

75 This is a perfect reason why all Five Basics are mutually inclusive, meaning, must have them all, all work together, and are not reducible, in my mind, to less than these; they are already distilled down to a concentrated list. Because in order to understand the ego's agenda of separation, you must understand that Ultimately there is no separation; and then to ensure the ego doesn't make a counterfeit out of the Ultimate and create a pathologically abusive spiritual subpersonality, you must Take Responsibility and understand Who You Are! See?

76 To be sure you get it: Relatively, the stitches and seams and details are boundaries that make the quilt beautiful and unique. Ultimately, the stitches and seams and everything else are made of the same "quiltness." As long as you understand this important clarification, you can extend and bend the analogy however you like.

77 Romans 8:31 (RSV): "...If God is for us, who is against us?"—and the Heavenly Father Hologram is for everyone (this is not a dogmatic statement).

78 Again, we are talking Ultimates. Just as the ego itself can make a counterfeit out of any Ultimate realization (like the boundary thing), it can also falsely interpret this to mean we shouldn't do anything about evil in the world, or into an apathetic que será será. The authoritarian abuse of God's will is unfortunately one of the most severe wounds inflicted by many of the Magic/Mythic institutionalized religions and their leaders.

79 And even if perceived as unwanted, there can become a negative obsession that ironically makes the unwanted part the most important to you.

80 The presence of evil is a rabbit hole unto itself, which I'm happy to go down, and do go down, in other places and times and from other platforms, but is outside the scope of our current study. I am not saying there is no such thing as evil. In fact, I believe there is; and I also perceive it to be perfectly part of the Tapestry, for now. Here, I am parsing out the ego, the devil (which is actually,

believe it or not, different from Satan and Lucifer and evil as such), and that embedded psycho-spiritual principle that acts as our challenger or sparring partner in life.

81 Others include any observable object or experienceable event, not only people.

82 For a brilliant and provocative artistic rendition of this theory, see the movie Inception with Leonardo DiCaprio.

83 Again, Romans 8:31, from previous note.

84 And there is plenty more to say about this, but insert your favorite word for Hologram (Spirit, God, the Universe, etc.) They're the same and not the same depending on what you're saying about them, and depending on what stage you're coming from. I'm not going to linger long on this point; so don't get caught up on semantics of the Divine, for now.

85 Again, plenty more to say about the dark night process. If you sense that you have entered this template, I highly recommend reading Dark Night of the Soul by St. John of the Cross, in particular Mirabai Starr's translation. At the time of this writing, I also have a series of videos on my website which you may find helpful, called "Dark Night Support."

Who Am I? (& who am I not?)

86 That is, everyone thinks they know who they are; but no one does. Or, everyone is trying to be "unique" and "stand out" which makes them blend in with everyone else doing the same. Or, in the freedom to "be yourself," shadow work is never required. Or, finally, identity is never understood to be beyond the body-mind-persona.

87 So, in that, I would differ from Ramana's one-tool approach, though it is said he also encouraged other practices as well. He was teaching from a particular system called Advaita Vedanta, which emphasizes the Who am I? question, and which is "transcended and included," integrated and contextualized, in the path I'm laying out here.

88 Imagination does not mean "not real," by the way. It simply means—again, break it down in the way we're currently doing—the place where images are made and held.

89 There are numerous websites and resources and books on all of these, so you're welcome to do your own research, in addition to watching the videos on my website which give a great introduction to the Enneagram and "Self Work" in particular (at least they're still there at the time I am writing this; who knows into the future when you're reading). But the books and websites that I have used over the years are The Enneagram, A Christian Perspective by Richard Rohr and Andreas Ebert, Human Design: Discover the Person You Were Born to Be by Chetan Parkyn and Steve Dennis, and Explore Your Hunger by John Immel of joyfulbelly.com (for Ayurveda). I want to make it clear that, in particular, I am not necessarily promoting Ayurveda as an example in this section for its dietary protocols (though they are good and I have effectively used them over the years myself), but specifically for the principle approach of "applying the opposite" to rebalance pathology, which is key in any personality-transforming system.

90 I am interested also in a deeper analysis and research of how the various systems overlap and intersect. For example, is there an algorithm that supports and points to the likelihood of a Cancer also being an Enneagram 9 also being a Manifesting Generator also being a Kapha Dosha and how to implement tactics and techniques according to this intersection? Or is it completely arbitrary? This multi-perspectival, combinational approach explodes the pre-scribed, pre-given, presumptive notion wide open while still maintaining connection with the idea of a template and the idea that each individual is 100% unique (which is a favorite insight of Magic/Mythic Christians). But, alas, beyond mere interest and casual inquiry with others who are engaging the work, I'm afraid I probably won't be doing this research. I'll leave that to any of you whose interest was sparked by this note; please report back with your findings!

91 Book 2, Sutra 33.

92 I would like to continue my conceptual/cognitive perspective regarding "no such things as opposites" begun in the Ultimates chapter based on the understanding of infinite relative spectrums that on the surface may seem merely like philosophical geek speak, but serves as a context for what I'm saying here about doing work to become a more mature person (persona, personality). On the relative "side of the street" (again, this is Ken's phrase, and from here on I will not put it in quotes or reference him every time), there are various spectrums of phenomena (e.g., spectrum of light, spectrum of sound, spectrum of emotion, spectrum of spatiality, etc). The spectrum itself is relative, because there are changes in degree within the spectrum (the Ultimate is "something else" altogether, as we've seen). However, within the spectrum, there are not only infinitesimally infinite increments by which to measure change in degree, but also, theoretically, the relative spectrum itself extends and continues in "both" (or all?) directions infinitely forever. It's just that humans are typically only tuned to a particularly limited bandwidth of perception to consciously register whatever it is (and all beings in all dimensions on all planets for that matter, tuned to their own bandwidth of frequency in the light spectrum, the sound spectrum, the emotional spectrum, etc—assuming that sentient life in all other dimensions and solar systems operate with the same constituent components). This is a rabbit hole that I am very tempted to continue down, but I will refrain, and stay on track here.

Therefore, the "midpoint" or "fulcrum" or "average" or "mean" of a given spectrum is entirely determined by the standpoint and perspective of the subject doing the measuring. All lines lead from a point. All numbers start with Zero. You are the Center of the Universe. All subjects are objects in the awareness of the subject. Depends on who's counting, who's looking, who's the standard. And the answer to that is always You...or, more precisely, I (it gets tricky when *I* am writing this to *You*)! In any case, from this higher level of cognition, it is clearly seen that there is no absolute center on any relative scale. The absolute center is only as The Ultimate Center. Get it? Therefore, back to our point, there's no such things as opposites. Let that sink in.

When we're kids, it's appropriate to think as kids, and to have correspondent cognitive training for that particular level of understanding; i.e., What's the opposite of black? White. What's the opposite of happy? Sad. What's the opposite of up? Down. But just as our elementary school education left us bereft of any interior connection or tools of interior cultivation whatsoever, so did our elementary school, or high school for that matter, education leave us at an appallingly low stage of cognitive understanding. We have to grow on our own from here, and because of "the way things are" in the world right now, that's not guaranteed or even likely. But this stuff matters, because cognitive development is "necessary, but not sufficient" (another Ken Wilber phrase) for transformative evolution upward through interior stages of consciousness.

Alas, there's no longer really such thing as "up" anymore. At all! And Flat Earthers, it's not flat, people! I do have a synthesized version of meshing the two, for another rabbit hole, another time, where it can be flat if you want it to be flat, or spherical if you want spherical. But for now, think about it... When you point to the sky, you're really pointing "out," not "up." Right? Outer Space has no ceiling and no floor. There is not even a reference point for whether the Earth is "upside down" or "right side up"—it's just flying through its own relative spectrum of infinite nothingness with its brother and sister planets and local star and the "universe" apparently gets bigger as it goes! Note again, relative, infinite nothingness vs Ultimate Nothingness; or relative infinity vs Ultimate Spacelessness. I hope it's sinking in, as you chew and digest bite by bite, lighting up glimpse by glimpse.

Here's another early example in the same ballpark as the story I told about the thought experiment I learned from my high school geometry teacher, and my subsequently exploded mind. This is from AP Psychology class in, I believe, 11th grade. We talked about a phenomenon that I can't even remember the name of, and I'm not going to ask Google (though Google A.I. probably just took note that I wrote that), in which, if you had, let's say, a dimmer switch on a light that did not have "notches," but was a smoothly rotating knob. If you turn it at the most-ever-so-slight increments, then while the light is certainly getting brighter, there is a point at which you *notice* that it got brighter. Same with sound. Take a volume knob on a radio, again, if it's smoothly turning, without notches or numbers, and rotates infinitely without reaching a "max" limit on the dial itself. If you turn it down slowly slowly slowly with the tiniest movements, it will indeed be going down, but you will not *notice* it until it has reached a certain degree detectable on the human bandwidth of decibel or sound-wave frequency. If we are to measure, the spectrum's gotta be chopped up somehow (gotta draw the line somewhere); and there seems to be both an intelligent, ancient archetypal template as well as a very arbitrary nature to the metrics we make. But the metrics we make make up our world in almost every way and how we understand ourselves within it. Sacred Geometry and Numerology are two really fascinating fields of study to further the understanding of the intelligent, ancient archetypal template part. For the arbitrary part, just study humans in all our random strangeness.

So, if there are no truly such things as opposites, then what we can talk about is *poles*. Poles within an infinitely incremented relative spectrum, with, yes, a midpoint, but again, a midpoint relative to the two poles (and the bandwidth). So we can no longer simply say "up," or "down," but have to say things like, "more up than..." or "more down than..." In medicine, the terms "proximal" and "distal" are used similarly. Because there is no true, fixed middle in the body, they use the attachment closest to the torso as the intelligently arbitrary reference point and say, "The wrist is distal to the elbow," (meaning further away from the torso), or, "The knee is proximal to the foot" (meaning closer to the hip, which is the intelligently arbitrary spatial reference point). It's an orientation guide.

What the hell does any of this have to do with anything that we're talking about, and so what why does it matter? I'm glad you asked. Colloquially, of course, we'd sound ridiculous saying those kinds of phrases; but the way we talk about reality is indeed how we perceive it. So it would be appropriate to update our everyday speech to match our current scientific, mathematic, and spiritual understandings. I had a student once ask if when the Ultimate Self is realized does grammar change. Yes it does. Or at least the thinking does. When there's no longer a contracted "I," who's talking when "I" talk, and how do "I" express that? If nothing else, here's why it's important: These cognitive gymnastics that I'm inviting you to attempt should be stretching your mind to infinity, and priming the pump for the jump to the Ultimate. But let's go back to the main text which is waiting for us at *pratipaksha bhavana*, or "cultivating the opposite."

93 The scope of this book does not have in its sights to go further into the following, but suffice it to say (as a "remind me to tell you later" sort of thing) that I have a few ways that I would like to "transcend and include" (to use his own words) Ken Wilber's work. His work is perfect as is, and through my studies and experience, I would like to now contribute my own unique perspectives and considerations to take it itself to the proverbial "next level." One of these ways is to add a third axis to his states and stages lattice. Typically, stages go vertically, and states horizontal. He does indeed say that you take your "type" (i.e. persona, mask, etc.) with you through the states and stages, and that it does inform your experience of each, but because I incorporate as a primary component in The Basics in general an entire self-work protocol (and he does as well), I'd like for it to be the z-axis, so to speak to the x-y. Plus, we're moving into higher and higher dimensions of cognitive understanding and creative contemporary representation in our world today, so why not make a cool

(yeah, I said cool in a published book) 3-D model of states, stages, and types that has a spectrum for maturity of the finite self. So Ken's stages axis indicates growing up, as he says; his states axis indicates waking up; and I'm making a mask axis which indicates maturity (that part of the AQAL transcended and included, and I have more ideas for the rest; those of you Ken students and scholars know what I mean; if you don't, don't worry about it...).

94   I realize also that this may be making you cross-eyed if you have no idea what I'm talking about; if you haven't seen my Enneagram videos, spent time with me in class, or studied the Enneagram specifically. But because I'm not dedicating an entire section on the Enneagram, rather merely using it as an example of "self work," allow my brief description to sort of give you an idea, acclimate you in the ballpark of what I'm saying and the approach to pratipaksha bhavana that I'm pointing to, and inspire you to explore further on your own if you like.

95   We'll use the plus-or-minus sign to denote "more or less than the word indicated, but including the word indicated as well." So body+/- will mean I have and am a body and not just a body, and at the same time I am not the body nor more than the body. Also, the more you engage this work, you will come to understand quite clearly that there is a subtle and profound and necessary distinction between "have" and "are." From the relative perspective before a realization of Ultimate Nonduality, saying (or believing, or acting as though) you are the body is detrimental. In the same way, when saying (or believing, or acting as though) you have a body, it is crucial to ask the question Who's speaking?, because if it's the relative self, which is a subject, and can claim to have a body, yes, but we need to be clear, and the speaker needs to indicate if they realize that the relative self itself is something that the Ultimate Self has (another object in the awareness of a greater subject).

Continuing on, in Ultimate Nonduality, it is seen clearly that "I am not other than my body." I'll delineate what I'm saying a little more clearly: When the conventional, relative self (identi-fied as such) who is not doing the work says, "I am my body," it's clearly delusional. When the conventional, relative self (identified as such) who is doing the work says, "I have a body, but I am not my body," we are getting somewhere, but still half-baked. When the Ultimate Self or Subject or Witness (disidentified from all previous) says, "I have a body, but I am not my body. I have a personality or finite or relative self but I am not my personality or finite or relative self," even better. When Ultimate Nondual Awareness says, "I am my body and my conventional self and That Which is aware of all of these. I am not other than, or I and That are not-two," *bingo!* Make sense? Good.

Now, again, eventually, when enough growth and evolution have occurred, the mask and the one wearing the mask become, not only from a Nondual perspective which is available always, but from an all-bodied experience, indistinguishable. At what Ken Wilber calls 1st and 2nd tier *stages* of interior development, there is dissonance between the character and the actor. When 3rd tier comes online, the dissonance disappears, and Jesus can say things like, "I and the Father are One." The relative self and the Ultimate Self are not separate, not two. "I and the Father are One" can also indicate an Ultimate 1st-person perspective in Union with an Ultimate 2nd-person perspective (or Ultimate I and Ultimate Thou are One).

96 For a deeper look at this, watch Jim and Andy on Netflix.

97 I cannot be certain if Ken Wilber coined the term himself or if he adapted it from elsewhere, but his most in-depth survey of the concept is in his book The Religion of Tomorrow.

98 As a direct recommendation, for an easy-to-understand synopsis, listen to his audio interview with Tami Simon called The 1-2-3 of God, produced by Sounds True.

99 from "You Worry Too Much," translation by Shahram Shiva

100 Though "nondual" is the standard term, and "transdual" is not necessarily different, I like "transdual" so as to avoid what Ken

Wilber calls the pre/trans fallacy, i.e., just because something is not dual does not mean it is the enlightened, Samadhi, Ultimate Nondual, or beyond dualism altogether. Transdualistic can refer to the "state" as well as a "neither this nor that, nor this-or-that" perspective. Not merely one hand or the other, but however many hands necessary to communicate the point. Same as breaking apart the idea of opposites. The black and white world of opposites is quite dualistic. So transdual is an Ultimate Awareness as well as a multi-perspectival "this and that and this-and-that" approach to relative, cognitive explanation.

101 This is not wrong. It's merely half the story.

102 For typically we are reacting to, responding to, communicating with what we perceive to be a "real world," forgetting (as we've already seen) not only who's doing this, but moving too quickly past the brilliant miracle of just this moment, just these things, just this presence, just this self, Just This. A tree. The wind. Breath. Sound. Coffee. A smile. A thought. Light. Meow. Words. You. Me. Body. Chair. Love. All just arising from nowhere, absolutely nowhere, and returning to nowhere, absolutely nowhere as it pleases. This is enough to blow your mind to bits.

103 Some say this curtain is thin, or has lifted, for some. But similar to out-of-body and near-death experiences, even if there is "memory" or even if there is "astral travel" of/to/from other places and times not confined to physical third-dimensional time-space duality, while it certainly points to something, for me it still does not prove the past, for the person is still having the memory from Here, Now, and filtered through the conditioning and lens of the present bodymind. No one has ever gone and not come back and come back to tell the tale. Let that one sink in.

104 Many examples come to mind: "For here we have no lasting city, but we seek the city which is to come" (Hebrews 13:14, RSV); Plato's World of Forms; Rumi's poem: "I didn't come here of my own accord,/and I can't leave that way./Whoever brought me here will have to take me home" (excerpt from "Who Says Words With

My Mouth?"; Isaiah 40:6b-8: "All flesh is grass, and all its beauty is like the flower of the field. The grass withers, the flower fades, when the breath of the LORD blows upon it; surely the people is grass. The grass withers, the flower fades; but the word of our God will stand for ever" (RSV); the Taoist "World of Ten Thousand Things"; the gnostic understanding of the demiurge which pieces together the illusory material world, as opposed to the real or true Creator-God of the spiritual world; even the new science that's telling us that the material world is actually nothing but space, and that there's really no "stuff" here at all; and many many more.

105 And it is pretty clear that the concepts in the movie have roots in the traditions aforementioned, including Gnosticism, which believed that "this world" is an emanation of a false demiurge (or lower divine god masquerading as the True Divine).

106 I am simply fascinated by this and do not mean to stir up fear. I do in fact believe that the "mark of the beast" in the book of Revelation is somehow deeply related to artificial intelligence, under-the-skin computer chip technology, and the takeover of extreme linear thinking (numerologically represented by 666) to the detriment of heart-based loving (numerologically represented by 7, the God number). I do also believe that the "good guys win," and now's the time more than ever to do this work to help achieve that outcome and usher in a New Era of Christ Consciousness (or the Golden Age or Satya Yuga, by whatever name). So please let the information I am now providing, if it's new or controversial to you, to either spark your own further study down such rabbit hole or simply take it with a grain of salt and move on with the rest of the text.

107 Philosopher Nick Bostrom is credited for getting the ball rolling on our most current consideration of this, though others (such as myself) have expounded upon his idea.

108 role-playing Game

109 I am not making claims about free will; that's a different discussion altogether that I'm happy to get into another time. The infamous

question about free will itself usually comes from a dualistic understanding of space-time, and separation from God; so what I'm positing in the main text is something else entirely.

110 For me it feels like "back," or "deeper" into my awareness beyond or behind the mask of that which I am not, and then behind that one, and then behind that one, until there is one which I cannot see behind but is the One I am seeing from, and is the one seeing through all the others (at the backmost of awareness).

111 One fascinating perspective that can point all the way to how twin flames or soul mates, e.g., Christy and I, find each other lifetime after lifetime, and the insightful intuition that we travel together as souls in groups which New Agers call soul pods or soul families. Who knows? But it's more feasibly conceivable by even the most staunch and sterile "scientists" than ever.

112 My paraphrase from Luke 11:11

113 This is another free will conundrum, which, again, I don't care to touch too much here.

114 Also my paraphrases from John 10:30, John 5:19, and John 16:23, respectively

Interior Domain

115 Which is itself one of his phrases, meaning to go beyond (transcend) the limitations of a particular way of thinking, modality, technique, philosophy, level, or entire system altogether, and at the same time incorporate (include) the essence, the good parts, the strengths, and honoring the existence, of that very thing that you are transcending.

116 I believe there are many reasons for this. One is that he has chosen, as everyone has the freedom to do, the lane that he wants to be in and the material that he wants to publicly present. He has made an indelible contribution to the collective, and in my mind is a living legend who will go down in history as one of the great minds humanity has ever been blessed to know, and that I was given the honor of having personal contact with. But he wouldn't

be true to his own word that his AQAL framework is not the final say, just currently the widest net, the most most Integral option for those who care to consider such things (I've heard, and read, him say this), if he did not encourage thinkers and seers of the next generation(s) to explore further. In keeping with his own groundwork, there's no way I could ever scrap the whole thing—it's that precious and precise and good—and there are so many essentials to include. But there are also some limitations I perceive that I want to transcend, and thus offer to you my own perspective (and perhaps in subsequent publications I will take it even further). I mean no disrespect. Quite the opposite, in fact—I would not be me without his work, and I am simply engaging him as he engaged his forebears. In no particular order, here are a few considerations:

1. Publically at least, Ken never brings the extra-terrestrial question or advanced ancient civilizations into the picture.

2. There is now cutting edge evidence (archaeologically as well as in religious texts) that shows there may have been multiple eras and epochs and "generations" of humanity on planet Earth that reconciles the conflict between literal-fundamentalist religious belief that we've been here 5-6,000 years, and mainstream science belief that it's been far longer (and the gaps in the holes of both stories). Ken makes a smooth assumption and has a seamless stream of (mostly Darwinian) evolution from millions of years ago to today. It's not that simple anymore, and the *way* his map has *actually* played out, both collectively and in each individual, is not as pristine as the theory (nor should it be, nor do I think he would say it is; it's just slightly misleading that it *will* be).

3. I would like to add a category called Octaves to his Stages and Tiers, to include advanced ancient civilization theory, the *Yugas* (or Cycles) as they're called in the Vedas, and the next frontier of human consciousness development that I believe have already begun to peek into (in the Upper Left Quadrant, for all you Ken folks).

4. If you know Ken's work, his States list stops at five or six: Gross, Subtle, (sometimes High Subtle), Causal, Witness, Nondual (which includes only two Ultimates!). As you've already seen, I have far more Ultimates than that. Witness and Nondual are two of the Ultimates, yes, but in my experience (and in the Yogic and Zen texts) there are many "Samadhis." I also can perceive an Ultimate beyond the Ultimates, a name for which I have not yet determined; namely, the Emptiness out of which the Ultimates come, the Unexperiencable Ultimate as differentiated from the Ultimates that can be experienced and have textures.

5. Lastly, for now, there is room for a post-literal interpretation of Scripture with the inclusion of ancient advanced technologies and siddhis. For example, did Jesus "really walk on water?" Well, Yes-No-Yes-Yes. Yes in the Magic fairy tale sense; no in the Rational, scientific understanding; Yes in the metaphorical, but not literal lens; and Yes in the siddhis and advanced technologies. Is God up in the clouds and create humanity? Yes-No-Yes-Yes. Yes in the Magic, gray-beard muscle man perspective; No in the Rational, evolutionary scientific understanding; Yes in the transcendent metaphor; Yes in the extra-terrestrial consideration. I know that's a shoddy rundown. More to come later. Hopefully you get the idea.

Alas, please don't get me wrong. Ken went hard at his forebears, transcending and including, and "fixing" the fissures in their models; so I hope you like what I do with yours, Ken, whether you ever get to see it or not. It certainly won't be from an Enneagram-5 lens (which he is), and will be in my own language, but I got some new stuff to say. Also, I hope that someone comes along after me, transcending my limitations, including the essence of what I'm trying to say, which is one reason I want to lay good groundwork now for them to stand on then.

As new information and new evidence and new science is revealed, we *have* to adjust our models and our ways of thinking and seeing (which is another reason why I believe there are certain gaps in his theory—he simply wasn't in the certain rabbit holes and alternative news avenues that I'm privy to, and used what information he had. It's the nature of evolution itself. I may write a whole book on transcending and including Ken, or just put it out there here and there. But I'll leave it at that for now. I love you Ken Wilber and am forever grateful. That's the truth.

117 And is it any wonder, considering the malicious agenda of the elite behind the scenes? Another rabbit hole for another time...

118 I want to make it clear, again and again, as a reminder, that Ultimately you're never not in the Present Moment; relatively, you can be conscious of it or not. And, there is technically a difference between the relative present moment and the Ultimate Present Moment.

119 It's also a-whole-nother subject to consider the possibility that ancient civilizations did much better than we at raising kids in a more balanced, interiorly aware, education system. Still, however, it's up for debate as to whether they were at lower evolved stages of interior consciousness evolution, in which case they were perhaps more advanced in some ways, and not in others... But as I said, that's for another time, and does in fact bring Ken's Quadrants into the conversation.

120 I recommend specifically Planet Earth II, simply because it was made later and has much better footage and videography. But both are great.

121 I don't care to go much further into this subject right now, because it's quite an entire rabbit hole unto itself, and would take us way off course. Suffice it to say, for now, that my trusted sources seem to be pointing to a combination between creation and evolution. So the great questions, If we came from monkeys why are there still monkeys?, and Where did the caveman go? don't prove creationism, and at the same time the fact that most have grown past the Magic belief in the gray-beard God in the clouds that poofed us into being once and for all at a time long, long ago doesn't prove the standard evolution theory. There are

problems with both, and there are even gaps in Darwin's theory, not to mention that he himself said he'd gladly concede if only one example was found that was counter to his data, observation, and conclusion—and guess what? More than one has been found. This is a fascinating subject that I have been studying for quite some time, and that is tangentially relevant to the work in this book, but certainly not centrally important. In any case, whatever you "believe" (because believe me, the verdict is still out, though we are uncovering some brand new surprising evidence), has no ultimate bearing on, and does not excuse anyone from doing, the work. At the time of this publication, my website has a list of what I call "rabbit hole videos" in which you can dive even deeper into this subject if you wish.

122 From Thus Spoke Zarathustra, edited slightly for inclusive language ("Humanity" was "Man" and "Superhuman" was "Superman").

123 Which kind of means a lesser order, or more lowly developed, being subsumed into something higher. In other, other words, the limitations of the previous are let go of, transcended, grown beyond (in this case the "animalistic" tendencies that prevent human-to-human cooperation and understanding), and the essence of that order is included in a new, higher order, or more highly developed—like, for instance, let's not kill and eat each other, or let's not deceive each other, or let's not take things from each other without asking or being given. Transcend and include is an important concept in Ken's, and my, work.

124 Or insert "oriented toward light" for "good," and "oriented toward dark" for "bad."

125 Transhumanism has become a popular word that usually refers to a "transbiological endeavor" as well, but from a technological standpoint; i.e., embedded computer chip technology, cyborg human-machine hybrids, consciousness upload to the cloud, etc. I'm talking about a transbiological interior endeavor.

126 I highly recommend this treatise, particularly Mirabai Starr's translation; Dark Night of the Soul by St. John of the Cross.

127 In my opinion (and who knows what Siddhartha actually meant, so this is my interpretation), the Middle Way, which some have come to call the way of moderation, does not mean a permission slip to eat chocolate, drink beer, have sex, use social media, watch TV (or whatever is perceived as a vice) "in moderation" (like Goldilocks—not to much, not too little). But rather, it's, "Whether you eat or drink, or whatever you do..." (1 Cor 10:31) find the stability of not reaching for or reacting to the conditioned or biological reactions or responses associated therewith. But that's not the end of the story. Only the beginning of the higher realms.

128 And remember our definition of a thing. If it has a beginning and end in time and space in any dimension or level, and changes or could change in any way, it's a thing!

129 For a more thorough explanation and investigation of sungazing, watch the documentary called Eat the Sun.

130 As I've said, stages is possibly the most important part of our discussion. In the same way as interior domain is the missing piece in the collective's awareness, stages of interior development is often the missing piece in the small pockets of explorers who do engage the interior; but it makes all the difference in the world.

131 And this, to me, is another sign of the simulated holographic reality of this place. For interior and exterior are both neverending, and are being upgraded with each new discovery. We have never found the smallest particle, we have never found the end of the known "material" universe. And it is all still held in the boundless gaze of Empty Nondual Presence. For a brilliant talk on the former, watch Billy Carson's "Fractal Holographic Universe Theory" on Gaia TV.

CPSIA information can be obtained
at www.ICGtesting.com
Printed in the USA
FFHW021442170619
53044260-58657FF

9 781478 779353